Joyful Witness

How to Be an
Extraordinary Catholic

· · · · ·

Randy Hain

Foreword by Teresa Tomeo

SERVANT
BOOKS

PUBLISHED BY FRANCISCAN MEDIA
Cincinnati, Ohio

LIBRARY OF CONGRESS CATALOGING-IN-PUBLICATION DATA
Hain, Randy.
Joyful witness : how to be an extraordinary Catholic / Randy Hain ; foreword by Teresa Tomeo.
pages cm
Includes bibliographical references and index.
ISBN 978-1-61636-810-4 (alk. paper)
1. Catholics—Biography. I. Title.
BX4651.3.H35 2014
248.4'82—dc23
2014030165

ISBN 978-1-61636-810-4

Printed in the United States of America.
Printed on acid-free paper.
14 15 16 17 18 5 4 3 2 1

• • • • •

For Sue, Monsignor Frank, and Deacon Mike
*Thank you for being the light of Christ to me and my family
on our journey into the Catholic Church.*

CONTENTS

· · · · · · · · · ·

ACKNOWLEDGMENTS
. . . .

I HAVE ALWAYS BEEN SOMEWHAT SURPRISED AT HOW MY BOOKS COME together in the end, considering my numerous family, business, writing, and ministry commitments. *Joyful Witness* may have been the most surprising of all, because the effort to gather these stories took more time than I calculated, and there were quite a few stressful days leading up to the date my manuscript was due to the publisher. The Holy Spirit and the prayers of many friends saw me through, and for that I am very grateful.

I want to thank Claudia Volkman and Servant Books for reaching out to me in the summer of 2013 to begin the discussions that led to this book and for Claudia's expert editing of *Joyful Witness*. I am thankful for the skillful guidance and energetic support of my literary agent, Gail Coniglio. Her encouragement and enthusiasm kept me going during the hectic days when writing the book became difficult in the face of other pressing family and work obligations.

I am very appreciative of the wonderful foreword written by my friend Teresa Tomeo. She is a perfect example of a "joyful witness," and she is an inspiration to many for her writing, speaking, radio work, and great love for the Church.

Words are not enough to express my sincere appreciation for the contributions of Jeanne Lyons, Katie Peterson Warner, Joe Zuniga, Father Roger Landry, Nellie Edwards, Staci Gulino, Manny Garcia-Tunon, Andy LaVallee, Tom MacAlester, Kerri Davison, Judy

O'Brien, Christian Moran, Kathryn Lopez, and Alan Napleton, whose stories are the backbone of this book. These men and women offer the reader clear examples of what being an "extraordinary Catholic" is all about, through the ways they live out their faith each day. I am grateful for their candid answers to my questions, their humility, and their desire to do whatever they can to serve Christ and his Church.

I also want to thank Monsignor Peter Rau, Kevin Lowry, Patti Armstrong, Donna-Marie Cooper O'Boyle, Tom Peterson, and other friends in my parish for their unwavering support and prayers during the time I wrote the book. This meant a great deal to me, and I am grateful.

I give my love and gratitude to Sandra, Alex, and Ryan for being a bedrock of support and prayer, as always.

Finally, this book is dedicated to Sue Fitzgerald, Monsignor Frank McNamee, and Deacon Mike Bickerstaff. Each of them, in his or her own way, played the role of joyful witness in the journey that brought me and my family into the truth and the welcoming arms of the Catholic Church, and I will be forever grateful.

"Wow—you must get to meet a lot of VIPs! What is it like to interview or be around so many famous people?" After working in the media for more than thirty years, these are still the most frequent questions posed to me in my work and travels. Even though I transitioned from the secular news media to the Catholic radio, TV, and speaker circuit in 2000, the questions still come up regularly. Now, however, instead of being asked whether I have met this politician or that famous person, people want to know if I have ever met a cardinal, or the pope, or the relative of a saint. Whether in Hollywood, the Holy Land, or Rome, it doesn't matter. Thanks in part to our media-saturated culture, there will always be a great deal of interest in those who are in the spotlight.

Don't get me wrong. It was exciting to cover breaking news and to interview senators, governors, and even an occasional movie star. Being back in the Church and on fire for my faith, you can imagine how it is even more meaningful and exciting to cover the Vatican and be part of a private papal audience. Getting close enough to touch those in charge of our one, holy, catholic, and apostolic faith is an incredible gift that I never take for granted. My work as a Catholic talk show host and journalist provides regular opportunities for me to meet our "religious rock stars," so to speak—and much more importantly, to learn something more about our beautiful and very deep Catholic faith.

That being said, I will let you in on a little secret. What means even more to me than spending time with a VIP who might have graced the cover of a secular or Catholic magazine is to meet and learn about those whose lives will most likely never be the focus of a front-page newspaper article or the lead story on the local or national news. I am talking about the everyday person, the everyday Catholic—the believer in the trenches who is going about the business of spreading the Gospel and building God's kingdom in his or her own unique way. My friend Randy Hain calls them ordinary heroes. They probably won't "trend" on Twitter anytime soon. You probably won't see them posting selfies on Facebook (if they even have Facebook pages). They are too busy being the Lord's hands and feet—and as Randy illustrates so beautifully in this book, they are all around us.

This is why I am so excited about Randy's book and why I am honored to write the foreword. Like Randy, I come across some pretty amazing Catholics who really *are* rock stars when it comes to taking their faith beyond Sunday and making a real difference in the world around them. They see a need. They have a passion. They might have been hurt themselves and want to help others who find themselves in similar situations, whatever those situations might be. These are truly joyful witnesses, who at first glance might seem ordinary to most but are doing extraordinary things for Jesus and therefore living extraordinary lives.

This concept of joyfully taking on challenging tasks with little or no worldly recognition is countercultural in today's self-centered society. Grab the remote and do some channel surfing, and see how many of today's so-called stars—particularly in the extremely popular reality TV genre—are thinking beyond the bling and the boyfriend (and that's putting it politely). They are few and far between. It's not too often that you see the Kardashians pondering the deeper meaning of life—or anything beyond their own belly buttons and bikinis. The world wants us to believe that our lives should be nothing more than an adult pool party: the culmination of one immediate gratification after the next. Maybe that's why these poor souls, despite their obvious material wealth, often make the news. But their stories deal with self-implosion, not exactly what one would call the proudest mementoes to snip and add to the family scrapbook.

Next, look at the folks on these pages who are so full of joy. How can that be, as they continually give instead of take? They are not out drinking and carousing all night or shopping until they drop along Rodeo Drive. It's not that they don't enjoy nice things or a good life in moderation, but guess what? Life is not about *me, myself, and I*; it's about *Father, Son, and Holy Spirit.* The individuals you'll meet in this book see the word *joy* as an acronym: Jesus first, others second, and yourself last. Their joy runs deeper than the fleeting feeling of happiness. Whether it's the father from St. Louis who wanted to do something about the quality and affordability of a good Catholic education or the young woman who was determined to help other young adults learn and embrace their faith, these folks are living out James 1:22 by being doers of the Word, not just hearers.

The only way to truly find ourselves is to lose ourselves in Christ. The Lord Jesus, in John 15:13, tells us that there is no greater love than to lay down one's life for a friend. The truth in this idea of putting others first and having a desire to make a difference also shows up repeatedly in secular research. Take the topic of volunteering, for example.

Just a few years back, the Corporation for National and Community Service issued a report entitled *The Health Benefits of Volunteering*, based on a look at some of the research comparing the well-being of those who volunteer with that of those who don't. Researchers found time after time that reaching out beyond one's immediate world through volunteer work is a really good thing for mental and physical health. There are social benefits as well. "Those who volunteer have lower mortality rates, greater functional ability, and lower rates of depression later in life than those who do not volunteer."[1]

Not all of the good folks featured in *Joyful Witness* are volunteers. Some have actually turned their passions into full-time work. The point is, instead of just sitting there and lamenting the state of the world or the state of their lives, they are doing something. Not only are they the better for it, but so are those around them. Their gift of self is the gift that keeps on giving, as that old saying goes.

Not too long ago I received a disturbing call from a radio listener. The call came from a retired man in his mid-sixties. He phoned my radio show as I was doing an interview with a friend of mine who regularly conducts seminars helping Catholics discover (or rediscover) their vocations. The call was disturbing not because this man was rude or angry. It was disturbing because he sounded so very sad and so lost. According to him, he wanted to do something to make a difference. He wanted to find out what God wanted him to do with the rest of his life, but he also thought it was too late because that train had left the station long ago. I asked him on live radio if he had any health issues that might make his situation more challenging. The answer was, "No, I am just too old, and it's too late." Despite giving it the old college try, my friend and I could not convince him otherwise. He was too focused on regrets and what sounded like unfulfilled dreams. In actuality, given that he was in good health and

1. Corporation of National and Community Service, *The Health Benefits of Volunteering: A Review of Recent Research*, http://www.nationalservice.gov; taken from the Introduction.

had nothing but time on his hands, who knows how God could have used him?

As you begin to read this beautiful book, I encourage you to ask the Holy Spirit to help you see more clearly how you too might continue to be used as a joyful witness. Pray about how to follow through on the sound advice in this book and practically apply your love of the Lord in bigger and better ways, to create a brighter world shining with the light and love of Christ. Reflect upon the words of a wise and feisty Italian American woman, Rita Rizzo—better known as Mother Angelica, the foundress of the EWTN Global Catholic Radio and Television Network. Despite the huge hurdles, professional and personal, that she had to overcome in order to start and continue her Catholic broadcasting ministry, she never gave up. She climbed over, under, and around those hurdles with a smile on her face, joy in her heart, and a determination in her spirit that would cause even the toughest of the tough to get down on their knees. As she said:

> I am not afraid to fail, because I've always learned something when I've failed. I'll tell you what I'm afraid of—and when I think about it I break out in a cold sweat— I'm scared to death of dying and having the Lord say to me, "Angelica, *this* is what you might have done had you trusted more."[2]

Now, go be a joyful witness—and enjoy the journey!

—*Teresa Tomeo, author,* Wrapped Up:
God's Ten Gifts for Women

---

2. Raymond Arroyo, *Mother Angelica's Little Book of Life Lessons and Everyday Spirituality* (Random House, 2007), p. 212.

SOMETIMES THEY SIT IN THE PEW NEXT TO US DURING MASS, BUT WE may not know their names. They volunteer for parish ministries, show up whenever needed, and spend hours in parish chapels, on their knees in Eucharistic Adoration. Others may be making a positive difference outside of the parish through community involvement, writing, teaching, art, mission work, or bringing their Catholic faith into the business world. They share the common traits of humility, selflessness, and self-sacrifice. They don't seek the spotlight and would rather see others get the credit. They are prayer warriors, diligent in celebrating the sacraments and devoted to serving Christ and his Church. They radiate peace. But there is something else that is striking about these unsung heroes of the Church. By the very way they live, they are shining examples to us of how to be a joyful witness for Christ.

Through my work as senior editor of *Integrated Catholic Life*, parish ministry, and my travels around the country to speak and promote my books, I often encounter these inspiring Catholics or hear stories about the work they are doing. I have spent the last several months reaching out to many of them and learning how they have become joyful witnesses for Christ. The practical lessons I have learned from them are at the heart of this book.

Joyful Witness: How to Be an Extraordinary Catholic is a book about these ordinary heroes who refuse to follow the siren call of our secular culture and instead keep their focus on Christ and our heavenly home. We all know, at some level, that we are called to evangelize and share the joy of Christ with others. But how? This book will offer numerous practical ways for ordinary Catholics to become extraordinary through inspiring stories of other Catholics, Scripture, and Church teaching. Each chapter will include practical lessons and questions for reflection to help us become more engaged in our faith. Reflecting sincere joy and the light of Christ to others is one of the most effective ways we can share our faith with the people we encounter each day.

These men and women are some of the *extraordinary* Catholics who in many ways are quite ordinary. This should give us hope that we will also discern how to grow in our faith and do more than the minimum required of us as Catholics. It would be easy to assume this book was written for somebody else, but I would dare say we all have room for improvement. Read these stories carefully. Reflect about what you have read and begin following the examples you encounter in *Joyful Witness*. Pray for the discernment to know what to do and the courage to actually do it.

There is an extraordinary Catholic in each of us. We are called to do more and lead lives of holiness, never forgetting that we are made for heaven and not this world. My sincere hope for you and me is that we will draw inspiration from the examples in this book and prayerfully commit to a new way of living our Catholic faith—a way of living that shines the light of Christ on all who encounter us, a life that can be best described as living a joyful witness.

CHAPTER ONE

These Children Are a Blessing
• SHOWING COMPASSION AND LOVE •

~~~

Those whose lives are diminished or weakened deserve special respect. Sick or handicapped persons should be helped to lead lives as normal as possible.

—*CCC* 2276

~~~

ONE OF THE FEW ISSUES MY WIFE AND I WERE CONCERNED ABOUT when we decided to join the Catholic Church in 2005 was how to include our oldest son, Alex, who has high-functioning autism. He was seven years old that year. Ever since his diagnosis at age two, we had found excellent therapists and doctors to help him function better at school, overcome his speech deficit, and cope with life in general. We were concerned about how he would do in our church's Parish School of Religion (PSR, the religious education program for public school students) and how he would ever learn something as deep and complex as Catholicism.

The first few years of PSR were a wonderful experience for Alex. He encountered kind and loving teachers from our parish who were patient with him as he grappled with the teachings of the Church. Things progressed at a steady pace until 2010, when our family encountered an angel named Jeanne Lyons.

Jeanne's job at our parish was to help Alex and other children with special needs participate more fully in the sacramental life of the Church, help them learn about our faith, and help them share their often unique gifts with others. Over the years I have seen my son blossom in his understanding and love for the Church, and it's in large part because of the heroic efforts of Jeanne. Jeanne is very important to Alex's growth as a Catholic, and we were overjoyed when she graciously agreed to serve as his confirmation sponsor.

Jeanne Lyons is not simply a volunteer with a big heart. This life-long Catholic from Morgantown, West Virginia, grew up in a devout Catholic home with loving parents and three other siblings. She felt an early calling (at age five!) to be a teacher, and she taught elementary school after her college graduation. But it wasn't until her own sons were born that she felt called to teach special education. Both of Jeanne's boys had challenges: Her oldest son, Shawn, was diagnosed at age four with Asperger syndrome (AS), and her younger son, Riley, struggled with sensory integration and speech issues as a child.

Jeanne shared with me the often difficult years of learning everything she could about autism, AS, and sensory integration issues, while her devoted husband, Rory, worked long hours as an attorney to support their family and provide for the expensive therapies their sons needed. Jeanne saw firsthand the difficulties her sons had in acclimating to school classrooms and dealing with peers.

Jeanne and her husband also witnessed their oldest son's growing disillusionment with Catholicism, after he experienced bullying during his last two years at a Catholic elementary school. The school administration had changed, and neither Shawn nor the bully was offered the guidance that he needed. The situation led to the Lyonses' heartbreaking decision to enroll Shawn in a public high school. This school welcomed Shawn with open arms, valued his gifts, and was willing to continue to provide the accommodations with which the Catholic elementary school had supported Shawn's academic success so beautifully.

Shawn's experience became an important catalyst for Jeanne's life's work in the Catholic Church: "As his disillusionment continued, I knew I had to do whatever I could to help my Catholic parish…be a welcoming place of refuge and acceptance for persons like my son, and for their families as well."

An example of Jeanne's creativity and the difference she makes in the lives of those around her is how she modified an established parish program called Children's Liturgy of the Word (CLOW) to become a teaching opportunity for teenagers with special needs. Typically a group of moms lead the children in hearing and understanding the Gospel reading during Mass in our chapel. Jeanne has set aside one Mass each month to be led by her group of teens. They meet the week before this Mass to rehearse their roles and become comfortable with their assigned responsibilities.

Imagine a teenager like my son Alex, who is nervous around strangers and uncomfortable speaking to a group, joyfully reading the Gospel to a room of young kids. My wife and I have witnessed the transformation he has undergone through CLOW. He has been given important responsibilities, has risen to the challenge, and has grown in his faith along the way.

With her musical gifts, Jeanne also leads a popular weekly program called Jubilee Music. This program is for children with special needs—ranging from Down syndrome to autism—and their typical peers. The format is a fun joy ride of songs, music, and games, with all of the children coming together for a special hour. One of the important goals of this ministry is to offer an opportunity for typical children to engage with and better understand their peers who have challenges. It also provides an opportunity for kids with challenges to model the behavior of their peers.

Jeanne is besieged with requests every week from children from local schools who want to come and spend time with her group, and she has seen for herself how the Holy Spirit has worked through this ministry. She related this relevant story:

> One Catholic school family that attends Jubilee Music, whose children do not have any disabilities, have asked for their children to be placed in PSR classes with children who do have disabilities. (Yes, this is a Catholic school family who also send their children to PSR.) They feel it's important for their children to have these opportunities to learn from peers who do things differently and to learn about faith, hope, and love in a concrete way that is unparalleled in its impact.

This desire to integrate and promote inclusion goes beyond these programs. Jeanne shows up at PSR classes, Bible studies, teen socials, and anywhere her "kids" are to be found. She works tirelessly to recruit typical kids to engage and befriend the children with special needs who are present, helping them to feel included instead of leaving them to sit by themselves, which too often happens.

Jeanne once invited three high school senior boys to take my son Alex out for a pizza lunch by themselves. Alex, who desperately wants to fit in with other teens, had a great time and talked about this special lunch for several weeks. This gift to my son, and to the boys who took him out to lunch, is just one example of how Jeanne Lyons helps young people with challenges integrate more fully into

Catholic and parish life. These thoughtfully orchestrated events and acts of kindness have a profound effect not only on the young people involved, but on their families as well.

To better understand the impact of Jeanne's work in her parish community and increasingly in the archdiocese of Atlanta, it helps to know what she is like as a person. Jeanne radiates joy. She is always engaging and full of energy, and she is a wonderful listener. When I asked her how this ministry work has impacted her Catholic faith, she described it as a form of healing for the challenging days when her sons were younger and not welcomed, valued, or included in parishes or schools. As she shared with me, "Having the opportunity to welcome, to truly get to know and to experience fellowship with persons with significant disabilities, as part of a loving community effort, is the very best, most concrete way to cooperate with God in growing one's faith, hope, and love. My job at St. Peter Chanel gives me this opportunity every day, and it is helping me to give this opportunity to others."

Jeanne shared a story with me of a CLOW session where one of her autistic teenagers—a tall, skinny young man from another country—did the first reading. He loves to read to the children, but because of his speech deficits and foreign accent, he can sometimes be difficult to understand. When he finished reading, a little boy came up to Jeanne and shyly whispered, "I want to tell that tall guy that he did a good job." Jeanne saw a wonderful teaching moment, and she asked the little boy if he would like to meet the teenager. The little boy replied with a sigh of relief, "Yes. Language seems to be tricky for him, and I think it might be hard for him to bond with other people, but I think he did a really good job."

Here is Jeanne's recollection of the rest of the story:

I helped the little guy follow through with our plan. I introduced him to our very tall friend, and he looked way up to say, "You did a good job!" My team member very proudly and enthusiastically said the most beautiful thank you I've ever heard, and he surprised us by immediately bending down to give the little guy a big, gentle, friendly hug. (Yeah, peek-a-boo, I see you too, God! And thanks for making this happen!)

When I got home, I called the younger boy's mom to tell her how impressed I was with her son's insight, bravery, and desire to reach out to someone who had struggles that were very different from his own. I explained that he had made a big difference that day in the life of a young man with a disability. She responded the way that the parents of typically developing children always do when I make similar phone calls. She said that being told that her child had been compassionate was one of the most important things to her as a mother—more important than his intelligence, his sports skills, and so on.

This only reinforced in me how valuable it is for Catholic churches (and Catholic schools as well) to be inclusive. Being inclusive is one of the most effective ways to teach our children Christian virtues. How could we not want to teach our children the most important things in the best way possible?

Some families with special needs children have started coming back to Mass for the first time in years because of Jeanne's programs and the parish's commitment to inclusion. Jeanne has even developed a sensory-friendly Mass space in what is popularly known as the cry room. This popular innovation has allowed families who previously could not make it through Mass with their sensory-challenged children to now participate as a family in a way they never thought possible.

What are the lessons we can draw from Jeanne Lyons's ministry and her passion for helping children with special needs? This remarkable woman—who wrestled with challenges at home many of us have never experienced—saw fit to view these challenges as a blessing in her life. What seemed like an injustice and frustrating lack of compassion for these children from the Church and others became the motivation for an education and training campaign to help others see each of these children as gifts from God to be welcomed and embraced. Jeanne says her dream is for all families of individuals with disabilities to "one day be welcomed with open arms into Catholic churches and schools who value them and give them the opportunity to share their gifts, living out the ministries that God has equipped them for in his infinite goodness and wisdom!"

• FOUR WAYS TO SHOW MORE COMPASSION AND LOVE •

Jeanne Lyons's story is one of overcoming life's challenges and learning to show compassion and love for the least among us. How do we follow her great example? As Mathew 25:40 reads, "And the King will answer them, 'Truly, I say to you, as you did it to one of the least of these my brethren, you did it to me.'" In reflecting on this Scripture and Jeanne's ministry, here are four practical actions to consider:

Embrace others. Look around you at Mass after finishing this book. Where are the wheelchair-bound, the people who "don't seem to fit in," or the visitors coming for the first time? Walk over and welcome them. Embrace them. Offer to help—and really mean it.

Love all of God's creation. As members of a Church that promotes a culture of life, we are called to celebrate the lives of those who may not look like us or act like us. Learn to see each person, regardless of his or her challenges, as a human being specially created by God.

See Christ in everyone. It may be easier for us to volunteer at a shelter to feed the homeless than to show love and compassion for an autistic boy, a little girl with Down syndrome, or a disabled person in a wheelchair in our own parishes. Look for ways to recognize Christ in each of them. "And whoever gives to one of these little ones even a cup of cold water because he is a disciple, truly, I say to you, he shall not lose his reward" (Matthew 10:42).

Turn adversity into ministry. When trouble strikes, turn to Christ and ask him for the strength and courage to make a blessing of it. We can allow ourselves to despair, or we can seek the good from our problems and find ways to serve him. One of the best ways to evangelize is to turn tragedy into triumph and allow others to see Jesus at work in our lives.

• QUESTIONS FOR REFLECTION •

1: Have I dealt with challenges similar to the way Jeanne Lyons has? How have I responded?

2: How do I interact with people in my life who do not look like me or act like me? How can I more clearly recognize Christ in them?

3: Who have been the "angels" in my life who have shown me kindness or helped me and my loved ones? Have I thanked them, learned from them, and tried to emulate them? If not, what steps can I take this week to express my gratitude and follow their model?

4: Who do I know who could benefit from my investment of kindness in them? What is holding me back?

CHAPTER TWO

A Little Pencil in the Hand of God

• IGNITE YOUR FAITH •

~~~

You are the light of the world. A city set on a hill cannot be hidden. Nor do men light a lamp and put it under a bushel, but on a stand, and it gives light to all in the house. Let your light so shine before men, that they may see your good deeds and give glory to your Father who is in heaven.

—Matthew 5:14–16

~~~

I FIRST ENCOUNTERED KATIE PETERSON WARNER YEARS AGO, WHEN she was a teenager in my parish. I have always been impressed with her zeal for the Catholic faith and the Christ-inspired joy she authentically shares with anyone she encounters. Some people have a "magnetic" personality, but Katie is something altogether different. People genuinely feel happier and more excited about their faith when they encounter her, and she is a natural at sharing her Catholic faith with others. This is a rare gift.

Katie grew up in a loving Catholic home with her parents and two sisters. Katie describes her early passion for the faith this way:

> Ever since I was in junior high, I have wanted evangelization to be not only my personal mission as a baptized Catholic but also my career. I was raised in a devout Catholic home,

but I received an even stronger calling to serve the Church during a profound heart-to-heart with Jesus in front of the Eucharist in the eighth grade. Since that time I have not wavered in my desire to study theology and catechesis, so that I could articulately and knowledgably teach the faith.

After graduating from Kennesaw State University with degrees in communication and writing, Katie pursued a graduate degree in Catholic theology, specializing in evangelization and catechesis, from the Augustine Institute in Denver, Colorado, where she graduated *summa cum laude.* She had worked her way through school as the communications manager for CatholicsComeHome.org. Her intention upon graduation was to use her speaking, writing, and teaching skills to serve the evangelization mission of the Church.

Katie shared with me that during her college and grad school years, the Holy Spirit presented her with numerous opportunities to speak and write—on a scale that was much larger and more frequent than she could have ever expected or was prepared for. She has spent the past few years writing even more and speaking nationally, and she now realizes that this is part of the "little role God wants me to play in the building of his kingdom." When I interviewed her for *Joyful Witness,* she had the humility to say that she has been "undeservingly blessed in experiencing what it's like to watch God's will—albeit sometimes his seemingly scary will—unfold in my life in the most unexpected and adventurous way."

We hear much today about losing our Catholic young people to the spiritual wilderness for a long period of time, with hopes that they will eventually come back. Katie managed to stay true to the Catholic faith, even through the tumultuous teen and college years. It is remarkable that this young woman stayed on the right path. How?

Katie gives all the credit to God. She says it has always been clear to her that God's grace covered her like the "shield of faith" described in Ephesians 6:16. This kept her focused on pursuing a relationship with Jesus Christ and his Church during a period of life generally filled with worldly temptation, insecurity, and doubt. She says:

> I knew...that I had to cooperate with that grace, and so it was in high school that I discovered the treasure of daily Mass. I made an effort to go really early every morning before school started. I have been a daily Mass-goer for a joyous ten years now, and I cannot even begin to describe the spiritual riches I have received over the past decade as a result. Daily Mass was a game changer for me. When I was looking for more clarity and purpose in my life, answers to God's plan for me, peace in the midst of school and work stress, comfort in the midst of social turmoil, and now strength to live out my calling more virtuously as a wife and mother, I turned to the Eucharist in holy Mass and in Adoration. I thank God that he helped me develop that habit in my teen years; I wouldn't be the person I am today without the sacraments.
>
> In addition to frequenting the sacraments, I studied. I studied the faith—all the time. I scoured books and Catholic CDs. I attended frequent talks and practiced evangelizing my peers—and frankly anybody—when opportunities presented themselves. The more I learned about my faith, the more I knew about it. The more I knew about my faith, the more I loved it. The more I loved my faith, the more I shared it. The more I shared my faith, the more I treasured it. Finally, I prayed. A lot.

Daily Mass for over ten years, devotion to the sacraments, passion for studying the faith, dedication to prayer—who among us (or our children) wouldn't be transformed by following Katie's example? What would happen if Catholic parents, through their personal example, led their families to the same kind of devoted practice of our faith?

When I asked Katie about the causes for the faith crisis among our youth, I was grateful for her direct answer, rooted in careful study and firsthand experiences from her travels around the country:

> It's hard to say it, and people don't like to hear it, but *parents* are arguably and statistically one of the greatest reasons for the loss of faith practice among young people today. Parents are meant to be the primary educators of the faith for their children. Not Sunday school catechists, not Catholic school-teachers, not the parish priest, but parents, and parents are dropping the ball big time. Researchers say that if you want to see what a young person's faith life will look like down the road, just look at the parents. When parents aren't living out their Catholic faith at home, their children suffer the consequences. They don't see the importance of the faith; their parents don't engage, so they don't. The home is meant to be the nucleus of Catholic culture, and parents need to take much more seriously their responsibility to make it so. When parents conform to the secular culture around them, their kids start to think they can live adequate lives without the Church, and they drift away.
>
> Secondly, our postmodern, relativistic, materialistic culture poses a serious threat to young people today, convincing us to adhere to "moral therapeutic deism," which makes the central goal of life to feel good about oneself rather than to

follow the path that Jesus Christ has for us, which is the only path that can offer us true happiness. Additionally, parishes around the country are facing huge deficits in trained youth ministers. The vast majority of parishes don't have a full-time youth minister at all. Finally, Catholic schools are now often places where young people say their faith is lost rather than nurtured.

All of these factors ultimately contribute to a weakened experience of authentic Catholicism in a young person's formative years. This makes it easier for young people to simply disengage when they confront the shallowness of their faith, marry outside the Church, fail to have their questions and doubts addressed, misunderstand the Church's teachings on moral issues or the significance of the Mass, and so on.

Katie's own parents have been very influential in nurturing and encouraging her spiritual life. Her father, Tom Peterson, is well-known for the evangelization work he does in helping invite souls home to the Catholic Church through TV commercials from the Catholics Come Home apostolate. Countless babies have been saved from abortion through pro-life TV commercials from his VirtueMedia.org ministry. Katie witnessed her father go from being a successful, wealthy businessman to a pro-life and Catholic ministry founder; this taught her from a young age that God has extraordinary plans for our lives if we are willing to say yes to his call.

However, Katie says the hidden hero of her home is her mother, Tricia. "I have never met anyone more prayerful, more trusting, more deeply in love with Jesus Christ in the most humble and profound way. She is a model of offering up sufferings to our Lord and laying one's life entirely in his hands. Every day she teaches me something more about love and joy, and she, in my eyes, is a living saint."

I asked Katie how we can do a better job of engaging our Catholic youth and helping them get back on track. She offered four specific actions for us to consider:

You simply can't love the *whys* of Catholicism before you love the *Who*. Many young Catholics today have been catechized without being evangelized. They haven't truly encountered an authentic relationship with Jesus or his Church, so all of the teachings and practices of the faith fall on deaf, uninterested ears. You simply can't love the *whys* of Catholicism before you love the *Who*. Young people need to be re-evangelized. In the past few years, I've traveled to many Catholic groups to convince younger and older adults alike that *they* (and by that I mean *we*—each and every baptized Catholic) are the ones tasked with evangelizing young people.

We need to become more convincing disciples of Christ. We need to talk more candidly about our Catholic faith when the Holy Spirit presents us with opportunities to do so (which is frequently when we ask him to). We need to make love for young people our primary motivation and develop relationships—not just simple one-time evangelistic moments—with them through discipleship. We need to listen carefully and discerningly to their doubts and their reasons for leaving or wanting to leave the Church, keeping in mind that the reasons they give are not often the real reasons keeping them at bay. This might require us to do a little digging to get to the root cause, so that we can effectively evangelize them "where they are at." We need to play offense, not just defense; we need to ask questions, not just answer them.

We need to pray like crazy. We should make it our daily mission to pray—through rosaries, chaplets, fasting, and heartfelt love notes to God—for the souls of our young people, particularly for the young individuals he has entrusted to our care in some way.

Exhibit authenticity and joy. There is so much inauthenticity in our lives today: pseudo relationships through social media, a constant barrage of advertising, false images of beauty and happiness on TV and in magazines—all aimed directly at young people. They need something that is real, and they need us to be the ones to show them that "realness."

Second (and my personal favorite) is the exhibition of joy—true, unbridled joy. I have had, thanks be to God, many people tell me that, even more than what I say about my faith, they notice the joy with which I say it. Joy is contagious. Be joyful, and you will spread joy. Be joyful about your *faith*, and your Catholic faith will catch fire in the lives of those you evangelize. Not enough people are joyful about their Catholic faith, when that is precisely the thing we should all be most joyful about, regardless of our age.

Now married, Katie and her husband, Raymond, welcomed their first son, R.J., into the world last year. Katie says that without a doubt her favorite ministry work is family life.

> Nothing in my life could have prepared me for the spiritual journey that is marriage and motherhood. It is, without question, both the hardest and most rewarding work I have ever done. Speaking, writing, working for apostolates—I love that ministry. But it's in building up the domestic Church that I have—that everyone has—the greatest power to change the world. My husband and I can model the life of the Trinity in our relationship and be evangelists to our relatives, friends,

neighbors, and coworkers simply through the way we love each other. Through parenthood we can raise little saints—the one or two or four or six that we may have under our care in our own home—so that they can go out and transform the culture in which we live. What a gift...and what a responsibility! The home is where the New Evangelization begins and the reason why it thrives.

As a young married Catholic adult with a young child, Katie is joyfully fulfilling the vocation of wife and mother. But how do her choices impact her role in the New Evangelization? What lessons are here for others facing similar choices? She admits the road has been difficult at times:

> Over the past few years, I have had to make difficult decisions that meant giving up jobs that I loved, places I wanted to be, and ministry opportunities I wanted to take advantage of—all for the sake of my family. Despite my usual uncomfortable initial reactions, when I make a choice that is for the benefit of our family, I am amazed at how God works through that. We grow in virtue, and I grow more accustomed to following *God's* will for me rather than my will for myself. No matter how hard I sometimes resist, it is easy for me to see—albeit often in hindsight—that his will always makes me happier.
>
> Dedicating yourself to your family often involves receiving intangible blessings, which can be difficult for people like me who are used to finishing tasks on their running to-do list, being recognized for a project well completed, and working in the field of evangelization (or any workplace for

that matter), where people can see and acknowledge what you are *doing*. Committing myself to my home life first—to my spouse and to my son—helps me focus more on *being*. I try to ask myself every day, "How can I *be* a better wife and a better mother today?" rather than, "How much can I get done today?" Transitioning to a mindset of seeing new growth in patience as a "job well done" for the day (rather than a work assignment neatly wrapped up, for example) is a regular struggle for me, but it's a struggle that I need and desire in my life.

Family life helps us focus on the people we need to become in order to be saints. What a training program—what a gift! When my husband and I pray together, when my infant son smiles at me as I make the Sign of the Cross on his forehead (and eagerly await the day I can teach him what it means!), I feel the indescribable joy that Pope Francis articulated when he said in his Angelus address (July 26, 2013), "How precious is the family as the privileged place for transmitting the faith!"

In addition to her vocation as a wife and mother, Katie continues to work remotely for Catholics Come Home and write for online Catholic publications. She's also working on her first book. This portion of Katie Peterson Warner's life well-lived will stop here—for now—but please reflect on this powerful image she shared as we consider what God's plan is in our own lives:

I've heard that St. Teresa of Calcutta once described herself as a little pencil in the hand of God. I love that image. We're just instruments, tools that God uses to communicate himself to others. I think that God has placed a call on my heart to communicate him to others—at least in some small way—through writing and speaking. Others are called to write God's love on hearts in other unique ways. But all of us are special inasmuch as we are his pencils.

• Four Ways to Ignite Our Catholic Faith •

There are basic lessons woven into Katie's story that are doable for everyone. Here are four of them:

Live up to the expectations of your vocation. What are we called to do? What is God's will for our lives? Katie experienced a call to evangelization after much prayer and time before the Blessed Sacrament at an early age. She later added her most important vocation as a Catholic wife and mother. We too can spend time in prayer exploring God's plan for our lives and responding to his call; in this way we gain an opportunity to draw closer to him and set our feet securely on our journey to heaven.

Be a lifelong student of Catholicism. Katie has been studying our faith since she was very young and has never stopped. Do we take advantage of the great teachings of our Church? Do we read Scripture, the *Catechism*, the lives of the saints, the writings of our popes and other great theologians? If we want to learn about our faith, we must be students of our faith. If we wish to share our faith with others, it must come from a place of deep understanding and love for what we have learned.

Recognize the power of personal example. Are we pursuing lives of holiness? Do we chase what the world offers, or are we focused on our heavenly home? As Katie pointed out, we have an enormous responsibility to model the Catholic faith for our children; they will practice the faith much the way we do. Be aware of opportunities to be the light of Christ and a joyful witness to your children as they become adults—as well as to friends, loved ones, and anyone else we encounter.

Be a Catholic multitasker. We're not meant to use our jobs and busy family lives as excuses for not going deeper in our faith. Work and family life provide unique opportunities for bringing our authentic Catholic selves into every area of our lives. When we set our priorities with God first, all the aspects of our lives begin to revolve around that center.

• QUESTIONS FOR REFLECTION •

1: Do I have a better idea of how to stay focused on growing my Catholic faith after reading Katie's story? What resonated most with me?

2: Am I making any excuses for how I live out my Catholic faith? If so, what are the areas of stress—work, family, or other—that I use as reasons for holding back? How might I lead a more integrated Catholic life?

3: How much time do I spend talking to God and deepening my relationship with him? Do I faithfully celebrate the sacraments? If not, what is getting in the way?

4: Do I know what God is calling me to do? Am I just guessing, or am I asking God in prayer for help and guidance?

CHAPTER THREE

"Lord, I Trust in You!"

• TRUST IN GOD LEADS TO AMAZING OUTCOMES •

~~~

Trust in the LORD with all your heart,
and do not rely on your own insight.

—Proverbs 3:5

~~~

FAITH AND TRUST ARE STRANGE AND WONDERFUL THINGS. WHEN things are going well for us, it may seem easy to have strong faith. What about in times of adversity? What happens to our faith when we experience struggles or suffering? Do we blame God, or do we trust in his great love for us? How many of us, when faced with long-term unemployment and severe financial difficulties, with a large family to support, with no support and minimal resources, would completely trust God and cofound an innovative new Catholic school?

Let me introduce you to Joe Zuniga of St. Louis, Missouri. Joe is the parent of eleven children and the grandparent of nine, along with his beautiful wife of thirty years, Jessica. He has enjoyed a long and successful career as a human resources leader with a particular focus on benefits and compensation.

I first encountered Joe many years ago, when he still lived in Atlanta. As I got to know him, I was moved by his deep humility and devotion to daily prayer, daily Mass, and the sacraments. You don't have to be around Joe long before you realize that he sees his wife, children, and grandchildren as gifts from God, and he views his love and care for them and his positive example as his gifts back to God.

Who were Joe's role models? He witnessed the powerful example of his parents and the way they lived their Catholic faith. Joe shared with me this moving memory of his father's funeral:

> As I buried my ninety-seven-year-old father this past February, he was surrounded by a packed church, with almost all of his offspring of thirteen children and their spouses, sixty-five grandchildren, sixty-eight great-grand-children, and a host of friends. It was a true testimony of his deep faith and love. This same Catholic faith has given me the strength to trust in God and know that he will provide no matter what the world may tell you. Having eleven children in today's world, as you can imagine, comes with a high price tag, but the rewards of being open to life have been indescribably beautiful from the first day of our firstborn.

Joe has experienced more than his share of career challenges over the years. Through no fault of his own, he was caught up in a series of corporate downsizings and mergers that created income instability and anxiety for his family. Although it was painful to leave Atlanta, where he had established firm roots in his parish and in his children's school communities, Joe moved his family to St. Louis a few years ago to accept a new job. Again he was subjected to a corporate downsizing. He kept busy with consulting work while praying earnestly for God to show him the way forward. Through it all his faith never wavered, and he had a strong belief that everything would work out according to God's will. Of course, sometimes God's will is not what we expect or even want.

Joe and Jessica have always been passionate about their children's education. In St. Louis they struggled to find affordable Catholic education for their kids. As they did their search and dove more deeply into the issue, Joe and Jessica felt they needed to seek an alternative to the options before them. After much prayer, reflection, and discussions with other like-minded parents, in 2009 they launched what would eventually become the John Paul II Preparatory School for kindergarten through twelfth grade. John Paul II Prep School is the first Catholic school in the country to adopt a college model: classes three days a week with the other days devoted to schoolwork at home. With the blessing of the local archbishop, the school has helped address a critical need in the archdiocese and offers a quality Catholic education at one-third the cost of the average private Catholic high school. The school began with nine students; today the enrollment is well over a hundred. The school's innovative approach is catching on with a growing number of Catholic families in St. Louis.

While establishing a school is extraordinary in itself, consider what Joe Zuniga and his wife were experiencing at the time. Joe was between jobs, with no solid employment prospects on the horizon, and the family's financial resources were stretched very thin. The stress of supporting his family through consulting and other piecemeal projects, looking for a full-time job, and devoting considerable time to the myriad of tasks it takes to launch a new school would likely stop many of us in our tracks. Not Joe. He took his struggles and problems to prayer and asked God for discernment and help. Joe felt that if God wanted him to be involved in this important task for the Church, who was he to say no?

Joe shared with me what he's learned from his struggles:

> The obstacles will always be there, and our fallen nature is to blame for our tendency to take the easy way out. I believe all persons can experience meaning and joy in their lives and overcome any obstacles if they let go of themselves and let God do the work. I have not had a real crisis in my life, at least not to the extent many friends have experienced. I have not had to bury a child, lose a wife to cancer, go through a divorce, or be stricken with a terminal disease. For inspiration, all I have to do is think of St. Teresa of Calcutta. I am absolutely humbled to consider how a poor, tiny nun spent her life picking up the sick and dying people—abandoned people—on the streets of Calcutta and giving them love and basic human dignity before they died. As long as we seek God first in all that we do and take ourselves completely out of the picture in terms of recognition and notoriety, he will bless our efforts. We must pray as if our very life depended on it...because it does.

What can we learn from Joe Zuniga's example? In many ways he is just like many of us. He is a spouse, a parent, a provider for his family, and a Catholic trying to do his best to serve God and the people he encounters each day. The lessons we can glean are rooted in Joe's humility, his surrender, his devotion to Christ and his Church, and his absolute faith that no matter what struggles he encounters, the Lord will see him through. Like Joe, we all have challenges of various kinds, but here is a man who refused to be defined by his setbacks. When faced with impossible situations, the temptation can easily be to focus on our own misery or think we have nothing to offer anyone else. Joe chose to look beyond his problems and take a leap of faith to make a difference in his community.

• Four Ways to Increase Faith and Trust in God •

How can we emulate Joe Zuniga's example and have more faith and trust in God? In studying Joe's story, there are four important actions to consider:

Pray throughout the day. Whether it's a daily rosary, grace before meals, a nightly Jesuit Examen, or praying with your family before bed, the abundant spiritual fruit from a rich prayer life has no limit.

Practice humility. We can choose daily to put our pride aside and pursue what God wants in our lives, not merely what we want. We don't have to worry about who gets the credit; instead we can be quick to assign recognition and praise to others, recognizing that we are working for God's greater glory, not our own.

Have clear priorities. We must be crystal clear about our priorities: God first, family second, and work third. This allows our faith and trust in God to inform and energize our vocations as husband and father, wife and mother. When we keep work in its proper place, we can pursue excellence in any project with joy and the desire to offer it up to God.

Love and serve. Let's love God wholeheartedly and love and care for our families in ways that provide an example to those around us. We should strive always to deepen our love for the Church and look for ways to serve. Loving our neighbor means doing anything we can to help those we encounter on life's journey.

• Questions for Reflection •

1: What opportunities have I had to show the kind of faith and trust that Joe Zuniga showed? How did I respond?

2: Do I ever attempt to negotiate with God over what I want instead of completely trusting that he always wants what is truly best for me? What happens when I do?

3: Joe recognized that he was being called by God to do something significant, and despite his struggles, he said yes. How can I face my own difficulties with the same trusting faith?

4: Looking at the four clear actions listed above, do I have challenges with any of them? If so, what obstacles stand in the way of my developing a deeper trust in God?

CHAPTER FOUR

Something Beautiful for God
• Using Our Gifts to Serve Others •

~~~

Let us not grow weary in well-doing, for in due season we
shall reap, if we do not lose heart.

—Galatians 6:9

~~~

A FEW YEARS AGO, I WROTE AN ARTICLE FOR *COLUMBIA* MAGAZINE, A
publication of the Knights of Columbus. When I received my issue in
the mail, I was struck by the cover image, a profile view of Our Lady
of Guadalupe, heavily pregnant with Jesus. A glow emanated from
her womb as she adored her unborn Savior-son. I wondered who had
created this striking work of art.

In late summer 2013, I was at the Catholic Marketing Conference
in New Jersey for a book signing, a talk for the Catholic Writers
Guild, and meetings with publishers. During the book-signing event,
as I sat in a room with several other Catholic authors, an endless
stream of Catholic bookstore owners, suppliers, and others came by
the tables to meet us. A few minutes into the evening, I looked up
from the book I was signing to see a copy of the beautiful image
of Mary from the *Columbia* magazine cover in the hands of a lady

waiting to speak to me. It was the artist, Nellie Edwards, and she gave me the print of *Mother of Life*. We had a lengthy conversation about how much of an impression her work had made on me, and I have followed her career ever since.

I learned that Nellie has devoted her entire life to creating, as Blessed Teresa of Calcutta would say, "something beautiful for God." This is not only represented by her talented artwork but also by the way she raised her family and through her pro-life ministry. How did Nellie develop her passions and come to know her calling?

This mother of eight children came from a large Catholic family in Washington State—the sixth of nine children. Her parents were devout Catholics who modeled the faith in word and action, teaching Nellie and her siblings the importance of prayer, obedience, perseverance, and generosity. Her dad especially taught her to speak out against injustice. At school she would defend kids who were bullied. Nellie recalls that reading Pope Paul VI's encyclical *Humanae Vitae* (Of Human Life) as a newlywed was responsible for her getting deeply involved in pro-life work.

Nellie and her husband often found it difficult to make ends meet with their large family, but they continued to trust in God, and he always provided what was necessary. While they stayed true to Church teaching and were faithfully open to life, Nellie realized in the late 1970s that some of her Catholic friends were using contraceptives, treating them like visits to the dentist. They rationalized their behavior by saying they could not afford more children. Nellie realized that the culture of life was in jeopardy in her own community.

Feeling called to act, in 1983 Nellie cofounded with four other women a chapter of Catholics United for Life. They began keeping vigil outside a local abortion facility, praying the rosary and offering assistance to young mothers arriving for abortions. Nellie describes the first day of her group's activities and the impact the Holy Spirit had through their work:

> The first day was the Feast of the Assumption of Our Lady, and one young mother who seemed to ignore our offer to help soon came out saying, "I can't do it. Because you showed by being here that you care about my child, so much more should I." Soon the abortionist's staff began routing their patients in through a back way, which made it all but impossible to reach them. We decided to walk into the clinic and pass out literature. We were cited for trespassing, at the request of the owner of the professional center—a member of our parish! We keenly related to Our Lord's betrayal.
>
> Because of the intercession of Our Lady and through the holy rosary, we were vindicated, and we continued our sidewalk apostolate. After four years, the abortionist finally closed up and left. (We knew of at least a dozen babies and their mothers who had been spared.) Our joy was tempered by the knowledge that women would likely go elsewhere. When we had moved to remote North Dakota, I had asked the Lord what I could do in such a rural place for the pro-life cause, never imagining how he would answer my prayer!

Before long, Nellie and her family began reproducing the small gift products that Nellie designed, which they sold to more than two hundred retailers across the country. In 1998, the bishop of her diocese told Nellie that he had given Pope St. John Paul II some of their ornaments, and the Holy Father had prayed a blessing for them by name. Nellie gratefully claimed the grace!

Eventually Nellie encouraged her four eldest sons to start their own business, even though it would mean a decline in the family's main income. The boys had all learned the skill of tile-setting, and soon they were asked to tile the sanctuary of an area Catholic church. The pastor wanted an inlay design of a harp and wreath of palm leaves. Nellie's sons asked her to create the pattern, saying, "You're artistic, Mom. You can do it!" Not being trained in this area but feeling inspired, Nellie asked for a PC tablet and a stylus in the hope that they would help her get perfect lines and symmetry. The project was a success, and this experience created a new passion for Nellie. She taught herself how to design images on her computer. Nellie remembers how excited she was to do beautiful work for God:

> After this, I experimented with the tablet and realized I could translate some of the sculpted designs I'd done into small posters. Some of my customers liked the idea, and I began to think that this was God's plan for us, to enable us to keep paying the bills! I had a lifelong dream of one day becoming a fine-art painter, and I had tried to paint off and on throughout my life, with less than ideal results. Little did I realize or even dream that the tablet and stylus would become my "canvas" and "brush!"

Nellie's art was woven into her pro-life work one night in 2007, when she was working on a poster design. She had the sudden inspiration to do a portrait of St. Kateri Tekakwitha. She resisted the idea, feeling that she didn't have the necessary talent or a strong devotion to the "Lily of the Mohawks." The thought came to her again the next day, and finally, after several attempts to ignore it, she decided to try. In three months she created an inspiring digital painting that five

years later would grace the cover of *Columbia* magazine's canoniza-
tion issue of St. Kateri. It also became the cover image for a biograph-
ical book published by Our Sunday Visitor.

When she was halfway through with the work, Nellie received
an invitation to give a pro-life talk at an annual Native American
congress. What was astonishing to her was that this group had no
idea she was working on the portrait of Kateri. It was confirmation
to Nellie that her work was blessed and that there was a clear pro-life
mission for her art.

Nellie's artwork is now used by pro-life groups around the country.
One that has become especially well-known is entitled *Mother of Life*.
It shows Our Lady of Guadalupe kneeling in adoration of her unborn
Savior-Son. Nellie says:

> It's thrilling to find out that *Mother of Life* has helped a young
> mother choose life! I use my artwork to evangelize—to point
> out Mary's role in the plan of salvation and, of course, the
> fact that we are a miracle people!

• FOUR WAYS WE CAN USE OUR GIFTS TO SERVE OTHERS •
Nellie Edwards's story is one of complete faith in God, a passion for
protecting the unborn, deep love of the Church, and a desire to use
her talents to help build the culture of life. We may not all be artists,
but can we not also create something beautiful for God? Here are
four ways to prayerfully consider:

Listen to the Lord. We can ask Jesus for help and seek his guidance
in our lives, and then we can listen for his wise and gentle voice. We're
not supposed to do all the talking; we have to really listen for that
"still, small voice" (1 Kings 19:12), so we can discern what he might
be asking of us.

Hold nothing back. Be 100 percent! Don't debate with God or hold anything back. When we have an opportunity to serve him, let's make sure we give our all and trust that he will never let us down. Just as does Nellie, we know that our faithfulness will be rewarded one day in heaven. Let's be "all in" instead of living for the moment or squandering our talents on things that don't matter.

Get involved. Specifically, get involved in the pro-life movement. Our prayers and our actions are desperately needed. Consider joining 40 Days for Life—be a peaceful, prayerful presence at locations where abortions are performed. (Only trained people actually offer assistance to those arriving for abortions, so don't worry about that.) Visit websites like those of American Life League, Priests for Life, Human Life International, and National Right to Life to become better informed, especially on the basics about fetal development and the history of how abortion became legal. We can also help elect pro-life candidates to public office.

Be good stewards of your gifts and talents. Everyone has gifts, even if they are not obvious at times. Let's pray for discernment, that we will come to understand our own gifts and talents and use them to serve God. If we all dedicate our lives to using our gifts fully to serve him and those in need around us, the world will be transformed.

• QUESTIONS FOR REFLECTION •

1: Where have I had an opportunity to create something beautiful for God in my life? How did I respond? How might God be calling me to create something beautiful at this time in my life?

2: Do I have a sense for what gifts God has given me and how I might use them for his purpose? In my prayers, am I asking for discernment and direction? Am I listening for his voice, or am I distracted?

3: How do I feel about pro-life ministry? Am I willing to get (more) involved? Is there anything holding me back from fighting for the defenseless unborn?

4: Do I ever consider my daily work as a gift to God? In what way? And if not, why not?

CHAPTER FIVE

Living in the Truth of Our Catholic Faith
• GOD IS ASKING SOMETHING HEROIC OF US •

~~~

The disciple of Christ consents to "live in the truth," that is, in the simplicity of a life in conformity with the Lord's example, abiding in his truth. "If we say we have fellowship with him while we walk in darkness, we lie and do not live according to the truth."

—*CCC* 2470, quoting 1 John 1:6

~~~

I FIRST INTERACTED WITH FR. ROGER LANDRY IN EARLY 2010, WHEN Deacon Mike Bickerstaff and I were seeking Catholic writers for our new *Integrated Catholic Life* website. I came across an online article written by Fr. Landry that impressed me. This Catholic priest wrote with great clarity about the truth of our Catholic faith, and I became an immediate fan of his writing.

It would be perfectly reasonable for you to ask, "What is so special about a Catholic priest sharing the truth of our faith?" That is a fair question, but I included Fr. Landry in this book because of his humility, his obvious devotion to Christ, his love of the Church, and his exemplary priesthood. He is also a gifted teacher whose writing, homilies, speaking, and spiritual retreats are feeding countless Catholics who want to go deeper and grow in their faith.

This native of Lowell, Massachusetts, grew up in a devout Catholic home with three siblings. At the age of four, he "discerned" the first hints of his vocation to the priesthood while observing his parish priest during Mass. He remembers thinking to himself, *The priest must be the luckiest man in the whole world—capable of holding God in his fingertips and giving him to others.* Later, while attending Harvard University and still considering the priesthood, he met a couple of Opus Dei priests at an off-campus Catholic study center. These faithful priests challenged, encouraged, and helped Fr. Landry gain more clarity about his calling. In his senior year at Harvard, the call to holiness became clear to him:

> By that point, I had recognized that my principal vocation was the fundamental calling of every disciple: to be a saint, to allow God's love to become the defining reality of my life, and to allow that love to overflow back to God and toward others. The question of what God was asking of me in terms of a state of life in the Church was secondary to this call to holiness. And so I decided to entrust myself totally to God and just ask him for the graces to take this primary vocation seriously, because I was feeling the pressure to prepare for what would happen after college—whether medical school, or political work advancing the pro-life cause, or something else.

Shortly after this epiphany, he prayed a novena to the Blessed Virgin, to whom he had consecrated his vocation, and he said this prayer each day after he received Holy Communion: "Lord, whether you want me to be a priest, a garbage collector, or anything else, please give me the vocation to do it with the spirit and the fervor of the saints." On the ninth day of the novena, unexpectedly, while sitting in a quiet chapel, God gave him the answer within. He was being called to the priesthood. Fr. Landry says this filled him with a sense of peace and conviction that he has never lost, despite the challenges and crosses encountered along the way.

Fr. Landry was officially ordained a priest by then Bishop Sean O'Malley in 1999. After spending several years in Rome to further his education, ministering in various parishes and schools, and serving as executive editor of the weekly diocesan newspaper in Fall River, Massachusetts, Fr. Landry is now the pastor of St. Bernadette Parish in Fall River and also serves as the national chaplain for Catholic Voices USA. When I interviewed him for *Joyful Witness*, I asked him why so many of us fall short of living in the truth of our Catholic faith. Here is his candid response:

> I long for the day when every Catholic priest—and every Catholic disciple—will be known as someone who "lives in the truth of our Catholic faith!" I think it's a minimal expectation and the path of true happiness, not a dry martyrdom!
>
> Even among practicing Catholics today, it can seem that God is asking something heroic of us when he commands us to put him first by praying each day, watching our language, worshiping him at Mass on Sunday, reverencing gratefully those who gave us life, doing no harm to our neighbors, loving rather than using others sexually, respecting others' property, telling the truth, and being happy rather than envious at another's good fortune.
>
> But consider the culture in which the Church is now seeking to proclaim the Gospel with freshness—where what

was once the minimum has become the maximum, and what was once routine has become radical. In a sense, however, that's a great place to be starting the New Evangelization, because we can't presume the building blocks any longer. We need to lay those foundations. And if we can get people excited about the pillars and laying them correctly, then it's much easier later to build.

What makes Fr. Landry stand out is the challenging yet loving message he delivers whenever he discusses our Catholic faith. There is no ambiguity, no gray area. He loves Christ and his Church, has studied our faith for many years, and is determined to live out his priestly vocation to the fullest. He is focused on our heavenly home and desires to help as many people get there as possible. In our own lives as laypeople, can we see the obvious benefits of focus, clarity, love for Christ that knows no limits, and a sincere desire to serve him and those around us?

When I asked Fr. Landry how he encourages his parishioners and others he encounters to live in the truth of our faith, he shared five ways in particular:

He preaches the Gospel as "Good News" rather than "bad news." Jesus said, "You will know the truth, and the truth will make you free" (John 8:32). The truth that God has revealed is not only splendid but genuinely liberating. So often people look at Jesus's more challenging truths as moral and existential straightjackets, but they're exactly the opposite. In Jesus Christ, God has given us a map to find the greatest treasure ever, the answer key to the greatest questions any human being has asked. The Good News really *is* good news.

He presents the real Jesus. Rather than present a domesticated version of Jesus that is lifeless, boring, and unchallenging, Fr. Landry invites people to come to know "the real Jesus":

> The real Jesus was radically countercultural and unbelievably attractive. He had crowds following up and down the shore of the Sea of Galilee to listen to him speak, sometimes for several days. They would carry their loved ones on stretchers for miles, just to bring them into his presence. At his word, "Come, follow me!" men would leave their livelihoods, their families, and all they knew to accompany him, not having any clue where he was heading.
>
> Once the idea that Jesus is a warm cuddly bear, who basically loves us so much that he indulges all our vices with a benign shrug of the shoulders, is replaced by the Jesus who loves us so much that he was crucified to save us from those vices, who overturns tables when we're being abused by money-changers, and who tells us to pluck out eyes and cut off hands if they lead us to sin, then it's easier for us to understand how Jesus would be challenging us with love to live in the truth today.

He always tries to feature the primacy of God's grace. Everything begins with God's help. He doesn't call us to anything without giving us all the assistance he knows we'll need to achieve it. He doesn't leave us orphans on our own. Rather, he stays with us and seeks to have us freely yoke ourselves to him so that we can reach those standards together. He gives us this help in prayer. He gives us this help— he gives us himself!—in the sacraments. He gives us this help in the Word of God. He gives us this help in the crosses by which we die to the world and allow him truly to come alive within us. He gives us this help in the example and intercession of the saints, especially those of his mother.

He strives to explain the *why* behind the *what*. Many times people reject the teaching of the Church because they can't figure out how it is part of God's love for us. They don't see it as an essential part of our happiness, how it's essential for our full flourishing. For example, if people think that "turning the other cheek" means allowing themselves to be physically abused rather than sticking up for their dignity and putting an end to violence without vengeance or retaliation, it's totally understandable why they would not only reject that teaching but also question Jesus's goodness and teaching authority in general. If people think the call to chastity for those with same-sex attractions means subjection to a lifetime without love, it's understandable why people would reject it. When it's explained, however, as the means by which Christ-like love (*agape*) is able to purify relationships so that sexual attractions (*eros*) don't destroy the love of friendship (*philia*), then people begin to see how, though countercultural, chastity points to the path of wisdom.

Once people have a chance to understand the *why* behind the *what* of the Church's teaching (an urgent concern today when the secular media regularly distorts Church teaching), they're far more open to following Christ and his Church.

He tries to set an example of the Christian struggle toward holiness. Jesus never merely said, "Do what I say!" He always said, "Follow me!" Fr. Landry thinks a priest needs to do the same. "People might think sanctity is somehow easy for a priest, but I try to help them see how priests are among the devil's preferred targets. I talk about my own struggles to align my life with the truth Jesus gives us. Like St.

Paul, the good I want to do I often fail to do, and the evil I want to avoid I often don't avoid (see Romans 7:19). I remind them that I too mean the words, 'I have greatly sinned…, through my most grievous fault,' and I go to confession every week."

The Lure of Lukewarmness

What prevents us from living in the truth? What are the obstacles that slow us down or lure us down the wrong path? One of the major culprits in today's world is *lukewarmness*. Fr. Landry identified three causes of lukewarmness, and he stressed the importance of understanding these causes, because the remedy will vary depending on the cause.

1. Not being exposed to people on fire for their faith. Many Catholics just go through the motions because they haven't been exposed to Catholics who are giving their all. The cure for this kind of lukewarmness is falling in love with Jesus—and often that can happen by close association with someone already very much in love with him.

2. Satisfying the hunger for God with other things. Many of us direct our passions toward the things of this world. We become fanatic for sports teams, artists' music, Hollywood gossip, high-tech video games, particular political candidates, work and career, cars, clothing, jewelry, our golf handicap, or other worldly pursuits. These immediate passions can make us apathetic toward the things that matter most. It's a type of spiritual worldliness that can't help but leave us lukewarm, if not ice-cold, about the things of God. Jesus said, after all, "Where your treasure is, there will your heart be also" (Luke 12:34). And in the book of Revelation, materialism was named as the cause of the Laodiceans' tepidity (see Revelation 3:15–17).

For this type of lukewarmness, what often works the most effectively is something that shatters a person's vanity of vanities. It can be the diagnosis of an illness in them or in a loved one. It can be a sudden death. It can be the loss of a job or the breakup of a relationship. Any one of these things can help someone to see that what he or she formerly sought was insufficient and there's a need for something more.

3. *Allowing sin to reign.* If someone is caught up in a dissipated lifestyle—dishonesty, drug use, impurity, and so on—he or she is never going to be fervent. The only path forward for this person is to be set free from the entanglements that prevent spiritual growth. For most people, that's going to require more than just self-restraining willpower. It's going to require the grace of the sacrament of penance.

• Three Ways to Live in the Truth of Our Faith •

If we are prepared to live in the truth and pursue lives of holiness, here are three ideas for us to act on in our daily lives:

Recognize that God is asking something heroic of us every day. God invites us, as Catholics in today's world, to put him first in our lives by faithfully praying to him every day, worshiping him on the Lord's Day, respecting all of life, and engaging in other tasks that defy the world's seductive call.

Don't be afraid to be countercultural. Jesus was the ultimate radical, and his example is one we should follow in today's world. He spoke the truth, showed love and mercy to everyone, and kept his gaze on heaven. Fr. Landry reminds us that Jesus is not a warm cuddly bear who winks at our sins, but he is God made man who loved us so much that he was crucified for our sins and rose again.

Avoid spiritual worldliness. When the longing in our hearts for God is seemingly replaced or satisfied by the offerings of the world, lukewarmness is the result. We spread ourselves too thin, with our desires to have a more expensive car, a bigger home than we need, expensive jewelry, more time with our smartphones and the Internet, and so on. We should keep our focus on our heavenly home and the good things God has in store for us, not the temporary and false pleasures of this world.

• QUESTIONS FOR REFLECTION •

1: Am I being honestly responsive to God's call to be heroic and holy each day? How does heroic holiness manifest itself in my life? What, if anything, is getting in the way?

2: Am I ever lukewarm in my faith? Do any of Fr. Landry's three suggested causes resonate with me?

3: Are there Christians in my life who are on fire with love for Christ? What qualities do I see in them to emulate? How does their faith impact my own?

4: Am I willing to be countercultural? Am I willing to go against my friends, peers, and others in defense of my faith? Am I more concerned with pleasing Christ than with pleasing them?

CHAPTER SIX

Love, Mercy, and Healing
• OVERCOMING OUR STRUGGLES AND MAXIMIZING OUR GIFTS •

~~~

The LORD is gracious and merciful,
slow to anger and abounding in mercy.

—Psalm 145:8

~~~

I FIRST ENCOUNTERED STACI GULINO A FEW YEARS AGO, WHEN SHE invited me to be interviewed on a Catholic radio show she cohosts called *Wake Up! Louisiana.* In our first conversation, I was struck by her obvious joy and love of the Catholic faith. Since that time and after several more radio interviews, I have gotten to know more about Staci, her background, and the authentic way she lives out her faith each day.

Staci Gulino is the happily married wife of almost thirty years of Glen (whom she calls her "St. Joseph") and the mother of three beautiful adult children, Amanda, Jacob, and Olivia. In addition to her duties with *Wake Up! Louisiana,* she is host of the *Faith and Good Counsel* radio show on Catholic Community Radio. A Catholic convert madly in love with the Church, she writes and speaks about numerous topics, including women's identity as daughters of the Most High God and marriage and family issues.

By profession, Staci is a psychiatric mental-health nurse-practitioner. Formerly in private practice, with a specialty addressing the needs of women and children, Staci now provides consulting services in the community to those in need of information and resources related to mental health. She has a particular interest in offering support and services from an integrated approach of psychiatry and mental health and the Catholic faith.

Additionally, Staci is a classically trained soloist of sacred music and the founder of the Gracenotes, a Catholic band of ten musicians that offers music for a variety of retreats, missions, and other events as a means of evangelization through beauty.

Staci grew up in rural southeastern Louisiana under rather difficult circumstances, in a non-practicing Baptist family. She describes her parents' relationship and parenting approach as "tumultuous." Growing up, she felt very unworthy of love, and she has painful memories of those times. Affection was inconsistent and conditional, discipline was often harsh, and she never knew what to expect. "There was a lot of brokenness in my heart from these early years, which the Lord has healed so beautifully, and I try to offer hope to others by sharing the love and mercy I've experienced."

God was always important to Staci, and she desired him as far back as she can remember. She felt loved by him even though what she was being taught about the nature of God was not necessarily unconditional love and mercy. Staci shared her memory of that time:

> I always knew—somewhere down deep—that there was more to God than what I was being taught or how I unknowingly perceived him through my experiences with the men in my life. As I reflect back on this, I have realized that I was always looking for God, though I didn't know it

consciously. Though I wasn't offered a Catholic upbringing with the fullness of truth related to the nature of God, I can see clearly that he was protecting me, and he arranged my life and encounters in a way that prepared me to serve him the way I do today.

Staci's early exposure to faith was in a fundamentalist Baptist church, where the pastor and congregation promoted a strong anti-Catholic message filled with the usual misunderstandings and misrepresentations about Catholicism. Imagine her surprise when she met her future husband shortly after her high school graduation and discovered that he was a practicing Catholic! Staci admits to experiencing severe internal conflict due to the negative things she had been taught about Catholics; she had a hard time reconciling all that with the fact that this man was kind, gentle, and everything she wanted in a future husband. Despite her reservations, she continued to date Glen, and he eventually invited her to attend Mass with him.

For many converts to the Catholic Church, once they begin to study the faith, there is a gradual realization that many of the views they held were in error. That's what happened with Staci. Her eyes were opened as she spent more time with Glen and really understood more about Catholicism. Looking back at those early days in her journey toward Rome, she credits the Holy Spirit for taking her by the hand and guiding her along the way. She is also grateful for the role of Father Clement Monroe, a Redemptorist priest who spent countless hours with her in 1983, patiently answering questions and overcoming her objections.

One by one, Fr. Clement dispelled the darkness, quenched my thirst for the One I'd been looking for my whole life, and brought me into the fullness of truth by explaining to me what the Catholic Church really believes, as opposed to the error or heresy that I was taught. He was very much an image of the love of God the Father to me, and I thank God for him.

Devotion to Mary, Suffering, and Healing

Unlike some converts, Staci accepted what the Church teaches about Mary when she became Catholic and did not experience any significant roadblocks. In recent years, Staci has actively sought to follow the Blessed Mother's example and seek her intercession. She finds it difficult to articulate the depth of love she has for her and credits Mary's intercession for helping her through a frightening time in her life with her son, Jacob. He had gotten involved in drugs in high school, and the years of suffering this put Staci and her husband through were greatly eased by their prayers for Mary's intercession. Here is how Staci describes this painful period:

When I closed the private aspect of my psychiatric practice to focus my attention on our family, I began a rather extensive study of Our Lady. I felt this burning in my heart to know everything I could about her. I needed her as a daughter needs a mother, because I was in such pain at the rejection of my son. I wanted to understand who she was deeply, which I believed would then inform me more deeply about who I was as a woman, as a wife, and as a mother. I wanted to know how to be more like her. I wanted to be honed and formed by her. I wanted to emulate her—her humility, her meekness, her gentleness, her receptivity, her love. I wanted to be mothered by her. There were places in my heart that desperately needed a mother, and I needed the mother of Christ to mother me and help me survive what was going on with my son.

During this period of Staci's life, she developed a profound love and devotion to Our Lady of Sorrows and Our Lady of Mercy. Mary has become Staci's constant companion, teaching her and gently guiding her in all areas of her life. Staci says that knowing Mary more intimately has helped her to be more virtuous in her own vocation as wife and mother. "I live my life from the desire to be like her, so that I may be pleasing to Christ. The wounds in my heart are so tenderly cared for by Our Lady. I cannot wait to see her beautiful face and to feel her embrace one day, as she comes for me at my death and, I pray, presents me to her Son."

The great news is that Jacob recovered from this dark time of his life and experienced a deep conversion shortly after overcoming his problem. He is now actively discerning the priesthood!

Merging the Faith Journey, Work, and Ministry

Staci was drawn to becoming a psychiatric mental-health nurse-practitioner (PMHNP) because of its biopsychosocial approach. From a secular perspective, this method considers the whole person in diagnosing and treating mental health disorders and employs a very comprehensive approach that includes both psychiatric medications and psychotherapies. What Staci gleaned both from her practice as well as her experience with her son is that Jesus Christ is the Divine Physician, and he cannot be divorced from the care, development, and healing of the human person. In Staci's words:

Understanding the integration of the Catholic faith and mental health has become a passion for me. It's been an area of ongoing research and study now for several years, and it informs everything that I do now as a PMHNP. When you truly love people, and see within them the image of Christ and the uniqueness of their person, you bring that love and affirmation with intention and grace to each encounter. The definition of the human person that I learned in my secular training is vastly different from the truth of the human person as given to us by our Catholic faith. This is what informs me and moves me to love and to care for those whom the Lord brings to my path.

Staci's other ministry work is through Catholic radio, which she humbly describes as an instance of "God's wonderful sense of humor." She never dreamed of a secondary career in radio, but she is grateful to God for always moving her beyond her comfort zone to serve in ways she never thought possible.

Staci was asked to join Catholic Community Radio in 2012, and it's been interesting to see how her training in psychiatry, psychopharmacology, psychotherapy, critical thinking, research, and communication is transferable to the media world—something she never before entertained or even desired. Not long after Staci joined the morning program, she was asked to develop a new show that would offer topics in her core area of expertise, directed largely to an audience of women. She prayed about the name of the new show and came up with *Faith and Good Counsel*, and she chose Our Lady of Good Counsel as the patroness of the show. Topics such as anxiety, depression, marriage, relationships, raising special needs children, raising virtuous children, authentic masculinity and femininity, and pornography are all addressed in a conversational format. Staci recognizes the Holy Spirit at work through the program because of the large numbers of people who contact her—people who might not seek out therapy but will listen to the radio. Her prayer is that the show will continue to bring help and comfort to those who are struggling.

Balancing Faith and Life

Staci works to keep life simple. She tries to live an integrated Catholic life, with Christ at the center of everything she does. She prays daily and places all major decisions before Jesus, asking for strength and guidance. She immerses herself in the sacramental life of the Church and all that it offers. She makes a habit of being grateful for both the blessings and the sorrows each day brings. She says:

> This level of unity with the Lord has been a journey—and it's a journey that is not finished by any means. My desire is to go deeper and deeper until I draw my last breath. I am now much more prayerful and recollected in discerning what God wants me to do, whereas I used to be much more inclined to make a decision on my own. I have made many mistakes along the way (with the best of intentions, of course). But my faith has taught me that I am the created, and he is the Creator; my existence and purpose in life is to serve him through the gifts and talents he has given me. In all things, I'm meant to rely on him for strength, direction, and perseverance.

Staci also depends upon the example of the saints to show her the way, especially St. Faustina, St. Monica, St. John Paul II, Blessed Mother Teresa, St. Thérèse, St. Josemaría Escrivá, and St. Teresa Benedicta of the Cross.

One thing that keeps Staci firmly grounded is making her primary vocation as a wife and mother her first priority. She regrets not learning that lesson more deeply in her earlier years, when she tried to singlehandedly conquer the world. Looking back, she realizes that some of her decisions would have been different or discerned more appropriately. It wasn't until Staci entered into a concentrated study of Our Lady that she understood that her vocation as wife and mother was the primary and most important vocation in her life.

Staci believes that many women today hold the belief that they can do everything they want, because we are surrounded by a culture that is mired in self-orientation, individualism, and narcissism. This is so pervasive that it is rarely questioned, but Staci has seen much misery in the lives of women because of it.

> Women are so very unhappy, and they have no idea why. I truly believe that it is a diabolical attack on women—and an attack on the family—to usurp our true identity as daughters and sons of the Most High God. It is a continuation of the lie in the Garden of Eden by the evil one: that we will be like God. These are the messages that we are surrounded by at every turn.

Staci is obedient to God's will in her life. She stumbles and makes mistakes, but she asks for forgiveness and begins again. She practices daily surrender to God and consciously tries to practice detachment from the things that don't matter. Finally, she seeks to be prepared for and receptive to God's call wherever and whenever he issues it.

Staci hopes that her journey will encourage others who may have experienced less-than-ideal situations growing up or who struggle today with a need for love, mercy, and healing. She says:

> There is such an abundance of joy and peace available to each one of us through the Church. Christ left us everything

that we need within the Catholic Church to not only survive the crosses and burdens of this life but also truly experience authentic happiness that is only found in him. Tremendous healing has taken place in my heart and mind through the love and mercy of Christ and his Church and through the gift of redemptive suffering that is unique to our faith. Wounds that were deep and traumatic have been healed through a total abandonment to Divine Providence, and I am now a very happy, joy-filled daughter of the Most High God. Authentic love, mercy, and healing are available to us all!

• THREE LESSONS ON OVERCOMING OUR STRUGGLES AND MAXIMIZING OUR GIFTS •

Staci Gulino is a shining example of God's love, mercy, and healing. Her story is filled with great lessons on how we can overcome similar struggles in our own lives and maximize the gifts God has given to each of us. Here are three actionable lessons from Staci's story:

Seek comfort and help from the Blessed Mother. We can avail ourselves of the comfort, guidance, and intercession the Blessed Mother provides, and we can try to follow her example. We have an inexhaustible opportunity to seek Mary's help in our daily lives through the rosary, especially before we engage in life's difficult moments.

Pursue God, and you will find the truth. Whether or not we've had a challenging upbringing with an anti-Catholic bias as did Staci, we all feel lost at times or have doubts about our faith. If we seek God wholeheartedly, we too will find his truth.

Healing awaits us in Christ's mercy. Each life has its share of pain, but healing and an abundance of divine mercy are available to everyone. We can go to our Lord at any time in prayer and seek his love and mercy for what we have done or failed to do. We have the sacrament of reconciliation, by which we can be pardoned for our sins and unburden our hearts.

• QUESTIONS FOR REFLECTION •

1: When I face life's challenges, do I stubbornly go it alone, or do I seek God's help? How can I be more intentional about seeking courage, strength, and guidance?

2: Have I taken the time to discern my vocation? How can I give this the effort it deserves?

3: What challenges have I faced (or do I currently face)? How might I overcome them in order to serve Christ and the Church with my unique gifts?

4: How would I define my relationship with Mary? How can I deepen my relationship with her?

CHAPTER SEVEN

An Unquenchable Thirst for God
• Living Our Faith 24/7 •

~~~

"Let the hearts of those who seek the Lord rejoice." Although man can forget God or reject him, He never ceases to call every man to seek him, so as to find life and happiness. But this search for God demands of man every effort of intellect, a sound will, "an upright heart," as well as the witness of others who teach him to seek God.

—*CCC* 30, quoting Psalm 105:3

~~~

Manny Garcia-Tunon came across my radar in 2012, when a mutual friend introduced us and told me about the great work Manny was doing with the Catholic Association of Latino Leaders (CALL). It's a national organization founded by Archbishop José Gomez of Los Angeles to work with the Church for the common good in the service of Hispanic communities throughout the United States. Manny, a founding board member of CALL, serves as secretary, as well as president of the Miami chapter. He is also very committed to working with the archdiocese of Miami in helping the Catholic Church in Cuba, where the political situation is quite serious. Manny works with others to help fellow Catholics on the island know that they are not alone and they are not forgotten.

When speaking with Manny, one is immediately struck by his great humility and warmth. He downplays his involvement in the various ministries he leads and his impressive contributions to the work of the Church, always giving credit to others. He cares more about others than himself, and that comes across very clearly.

In addition to the various ministries he leads and his other Church work, Manny is the president of an international design-build firm headquartered in Miami, Florida. He is a business columnist for the *Miami Herald* and *El Nuevo Herald*, and his motivational business column appears weekly in various papers across the country, in both English and Spanish. Manny is also a business columnist for VOXXI.com, a leading news, business, and entertainment website targeting English-speaking Hispanics. Additionally, Manny has been a contributor on Univision's Miami small-business segment, *Unos Minutos Con Manny*, as well as on Univision's national morning show, *Despierta America*.

Manny grew up in Miami, Florida, in a very devout Catholic home. His family is from Cuba, having moved there several generations ago from Spain. After Castro's revolution, his family left Cuba in 1960, and many of them settled in Miami. The family didn't have much while Manny was growing up, but they certainly had what they needed. This former altar boy recalls his early formation as a Catholic with fond and grateful memories:

> The quality of our education was phenomenal all around, but our spiritual formation in particular and our preparation for the sacraments was spectacular. I owe so much of my faith to those days and the true "partnership" that existed between the faith I was truly living at home and the faith I was learning in school. I still believe that that's the formula

that works best. My faith has always been with me, and in me, and a part of me.

Manny says he has always had an unquenchable thirst for God. He describes it as a desire to know him more intimately on a deeply personal level and to serve him in any way possible. He credits this to the fact that he was blessed to experience God through his family, community, and parish life, but Manny has always felt an "extra" call to do more for God. In his youth, this manifested itself in his service as an altar boy, then as an usher, and eventually as an assistant retreat leader. Manny has used his lifelong love of music to serve God, becoming a cantor at age fifteen and later forming a band called Rejoice. This talented group performed before St. John Paul II during World Youth Day in Denver in 1993 and still performs today, with Manny, his wife, and his sister-in-law providing vocals.

Today Manny and his family are very involved in their parish, where they lead Emmaus retreats focused on bringing others to an encounter with Christ, as well as marriage preparation retreats for couples. As Manny reflected on his ministry work, he had this to share: "Looking back, I realize that service—putting yourself out there and serving God when and where you are at any given moment—goes a long way in nurturing your own relationship with him."

So how does someone like Manny, so heavily involved with various ministries, career commitments, and family responsibilities, stay on track with his Catholic faith? What sustains him during challenging periods in his life? He says it's his devotion to the sacraments, a consistent prayer life, strong fellowship with other Catholics in his community, and a love for the Blessed Mother. In an effort to avoid the tumultuous midlife crises he observed in those around him—who were experiencing personal, professional, spiritual, and emotional conflicts so typical during these years—he began to focus more intently on his spiritual life. In addition to monthly spiritual direction and confession, once a year he tries to attend a silent, three-night retreat based on the spiritual exercises of St. Ignatius.

With all of these activities and spiritual disciplines, Manny began to realize something: The Lord didn't want more *from* him; he wanted more *of* him. When a friend invited him to attend a retreat focusing on total personal consecration to the Blessed Mother, Manny knew this was inspired by the Holy Spirit. There he made his commitment to the Blessed Mother, a consecration that has made a significant difference in his life:

> I have come to realize that everything I lack, everything I strive for, Our Blessed Mother has in abundance: humility, patience, selflessness, complete trust in the Lord, brave faith, tenderness, generosity, indifference to things that keep me from God. All of these things and more Mary has in abundance. She is the perfect path to her Son, our best example of what it means to be a true follower of Christ. In the short time since my consecration, I can see my path to Jesus more clearly than ever before, as the Blessed Mother leads me by her example to love abundantly, sacrifice willingly, give generously, and live joyfully.

One of the areas I have written about extensively is the importance of leading an integrated Catholic life, with Christ at the center of our faith, family, and work. Manny has a clear focus on having the right priorities in how he lives his faith every day. Here is his take on the idea of an integrated Catholic life:

> I simply am who I am 24/7. Manny Garcia-Tunon is a Christian first and foremost. I am a husband and a father.

Then, and only after the above, am I a business owner, a writer and columnist, and so on. I believe it is so important that we not divorce our faith from our work. On the contrary, I want to help people encounter Jesus every chance I get—and I spend most of my time at work. I expect my business to be run ethically and morally. I expect that my employees and clients be treated fairly and that, as a company, we deal with others' needs with compassion and generosity. It doesn't always work out—you can't please everyone—but it's what we strive for.

Faith has had, and continues to have, a tremendous impact on my family, my friends, and my business, because it guides all of those relationships. My faith guides the way I interact with others, and that has an effect on the way they interact with me. For me, my faith is out there, front and center. I'm not "showy" about it; I don't force my beliefs on others, but I'm always ready to share my faith. If I am going to be true to who I am as a person, then I have to surrender myself to the fact that my life is the Lord's. "Belonging" to the Lord means that I must strive to discern God's will for my life and live my life for him. That means that every decision I make, every action I take—whether it be as a husband and father, as a friend, or as president of my design-build firm—must be taken with discernment. It doesn't always work that way, not even close, but it's what I strive for every time.

With all of the inspiring things you have read about Manny Garcia-Tunon's life and the way he lives his Catholic faith, there is something else that makes him one of the "joyful witnesses" the world so desperately needs: He radiates joy and the light of Christ to everyone he encounters. Joy is attractive, and Manny believes that, in order to be effective evangelizers, we must let people see our Christ-inspired joy. This is a choice and a commitment; it will be strengthened by prayer and living an authentic Catholic life, with our eyes on Christ and our heavenly home, not by getting stuck in the mud of the secular world. Manny points to the example of Pope Francis:

If Pope Francis is teaching us anything, it's that we are all called to live joyfully and humbly and be the light of Christ to the world. And he is teaching the world this by his example. Pope Francis doesn't concern himself with the frivolity we have attached to our Church. He wants to make the Church a mission Church once again. He wants his priests and pastors to smell like their sheep. He wants all the faithful to live joyfully and bring others to Christ. The joy of the Lord is our strength!

• Four Actions to Help Us Live Our Faith 24/7 •

At the root of Manny's life and activities is a deep love and desire for God, an "unquenchable thirst," as he describes it. How do we develop such a deep desire for God and lead more integrated Catholic lives? There are four key lessons to glean from Manny's example.

Practice prayer and discernment. We have an opportunity every single day to seek God in prayer and ask for his help. Instead of asking God to validate our decisions, we should ask him to lead and guide us where we need to go.

Stay connected to family, community, and fellowship. Our spiritual life isn't meant to be lived in isolation. Being connected in tangible ways with our family, neighbors, work colleagues, and members of our parish is vital to our spiritual journey as Catholics. We should see the people God has placed in our lives as sources of strength to keep us focused and grounded.

Seek out the Blessed Mother. Mary possesses everything we lack, everything we desire. She is always there for us, willing to teach us and intercede for us if we will only ask her for help. Most importantly, our Blessed Mother will lead us to a closer relationship with her son, Jesus.

Radiate joy, humility, and the light of Christ. Pope Francis is a wonderful role model for us all as one who lives joyfully and humbly as a light of Christ to the world. We can learn from his example and shed our attachments to what the world offers, thus discovering what a life dedicated to Christ can offer. If we live this way, we make the way to Christ and the Church infinitely more attractive to others, and we too can play an important part in the New Evangelization.

• QUESTIONS FOR REFLECTION •

1: Manny is well-grounded in his Catholic faith, which seems to inform his every thought and action. What are the obstacles keeping me from having the same grounded faith? Am I properly formed as a Catholic? Do I need to study and rededicate myself to a stronger practice of my Catholic faith?

2: What are my sources of strength when it comes to my Catholic faith? Do I see my family, neighbors, and Catholic brothers and sisters as sources of encouragement and strength for my spiritual life? In what ways?

3: How can I become more aware of where I am in terms of my spiritual and personal development? What might I do to develop more awareness and growth in this area?

4: In what ways do I make Christ and the Church look more attractive to others through the way I live my Catholic faith?

CHAPTER EIGHT

Investing in Our Future
• HELPING OUR CATHOLIC YOUNG ADULTS
KEEP THEIR FAITH ALIVE •

~~~

The Church entrusts to young people the task of proclaiming to the world the joy which springs from having met Christ. Dear friends, allow yourselves to be drawn to Christ, accept his invitation to follow him. Go and preach the Good News that redeems; do it with happiness in your hearts and become communicators of hope in a world which is often tempted to despair, communicators of faith in a society which at times seems resigned to disbelief, communicators of love, in daily events that are often marked by a mentality of the most unbridled selfishness.

—Pope John Paul II's Message to World Youth Day, 1995

~~~

IN 2012, TOM MACALESTER INVITED ME TO SPEAK TO THE INCOMING freshman class at Belmont Abbey College outside of Charlotte, North Carolina. Tom, a former FOCUS missionary, is now the dean of student life at this small Catholic liberal arts school, but at the time he was in charge of student programs. Belmont Abbey has a passion for providing a high-quality education experience for students in a faithful Catholic setting, and Tom's gifts of empathy, compassion, high energy, humility, thoughtfulness, and warmth make him a great mentor to the students in his care. Tom is also passionate about his Catholic faith and about sharing his love of Christ and the Church with everyone he encounters.

When I contacted him about being part of *Joyful Witness*, his immediate and instinctive response made him the perfect choice: "I am not worthy."

Tom was raised as an only child in Tampa, Florida, in a faithful Catholic home. Down the street was his parish church, where he attended Mass each week, as well as the parochial school, which he attended from kindergarten through eighth grade. In middle school and high school, he was very involved at his parish in youth and music ministry. Tom played guitar and sang at the youth Mass on Sunday nights, and he remembers this as one of the first times he realized his talents could be used for the glory of God. He belonged to a tight-knit group of musicians who truly understood the meaning of music ministry and recognized that they were not the most important part of the Mass.

Tom credits his four years at Jesuit High School in Tampa for forming him into someone who thinks of others. The Jesuit High School motto is "Men for Others," and everything Tom was involved in—from football, to band, to service clubs—served the mission of forming boys into men who put the needs of others before their own.

The summer after high school, in 2002, Tom was a youth leader at the Steubenville Atlanta conference and was preparing to attend Florida State University, his favorite school since childhood. At the conference, he met a Florida State University student who just so happened to be the president of the Catholic Student Union.

Through that encounter, Tom knew that CSU would be his home when he arrived that August.

The Catholic Student Union is where Tom's faith became something personal and real. Pope Emeritus Benedict XVI tells us that our faith should be "personal but never private." Tom says of the experience:

> It was the first time in my life I had the freedom to seek after the heart of God as he wanted me to. I had my first dose of real freedom in college, and I knew I was faced with a decision: get involved in the party lifestyle, as many of my friends from high school were doing around me at FSU, or invest myself in the men and women of CSU and grow closer to Christ through loving that community. By the grace of God, I chose the latter. I very quickly got involved in music ministry at the Catholic Student Union, and I also participated in youth ministry teams and led Bible studies, discipleship groups, and evangelization teams.

Tom's choice is one our Catholic young people face during their college years, but they too often take the path offered by the world instead of making the choice Tom made. Tom shared one particularly meaningful experience when he led a student retreat for the Catholic Student Union on the theme of identity in Christ and how to more fully understand it. Tom discovered that the more he planned and mulled over the topics for the retreat, the more he sensed God speaking to him and calling him more deeply into a loving relationship with him. As Tom stayed true to his faith throughout college, God provided additional opportunities for him to serve.

It was also in college that Tom met his future wife and got married, which he considers one of two "life-changing moments." The second was deciding to become a FOCUS (Fellowship of Catholic University Students) missionary after college. I asked Tom if he always felt called to be a missionary, and I was intrigued by his refreshingly candid answer:

> I sometimes struggle with the idea that God has just one plan for me. Do I believe that God has guided me, through his patience and mercy, to every decision I have made? Yes, I do. Has he made his will abundantly clear in some big decisions I have had to make over the years? Yes...sometimes. I often think of God chuckling when I am feverishly praying over a decision I need to make. I hear him saying, "All right. I gave you free will, and I will be on the other side of any decision you make. Use that free will and choose." If I can look back on every decision I have made (good or bad) and see God working his way into the picture and guiding the consequences, how can I think it will be any different in my future decisions?
>
> My years as a missionary with FOCUS were some of the hardest and best years of my life. As a missionary, we raised our own salaries by partnering with faithful people who saw the need we were filling on college campuses. If ever I understood what St. Faustina was talking about when she would pray, "Jesus, I trust in you," it was when I was fund-raising a living for my wife and growing family. When I would pray that prayer while working on raising funds, it wasn't a pretty, short little prayer to get me through to the next month. It was an honest realization that at the end of the day, all I have

is Jesus and the blessings he chooses to bestow on me and my family.

So when I think of God's plan for my life, I make sure that before I make major decisions, I ask the Lord. He has always been there for me and my family, and he always will be.

Let's stop for a minute and ask ourselves how many young adult Catholics we know are as committed as Tom to living and sharing their Catholic faith. I think the answer is a little frightening. I explored this topic with Tom extensively, and I came up with a list of "best practices" I learned from him that we can utilize in our own lives and our children's lives and share with the young adults in our extended circles.

There is a God, and I am loved by him. In each of our lives, this revelation will come if we seek first the kingdom. Once these two truths sink in, they become the foundation for everything that follows. Matthew and the other apostles all had sincere, raw experiences of the Lord. It was because of those experiences that they all had a burning desire to evangelize.

The single most important thing in life is our relationship with the living God. Everything about being a Catholic, being a Christian, is about a relationship with God. Pope Emeritus Benedict often spoke of a friendship with Jesus Christ. Many of our Protestant brothers and sisters get this. They realize that the faith is about a dialogue, a relationship with God. When we really look at the Church and her teachings, the sacraments all make sense if we realize they are God's way of calling us into a deeper relationship with him. If we only see the Church as a list of rules and regulations, we may miss the importance of an intimate relationship with God. But if we see those guidelines and directions blossoming from a sincere experience of the living God, our expectations change.

The Church is hyper-relevant in today's world, despite popular opinion. Many in the younger generation are frustrated with what they see as a Church that is out of touch with modern man. They think the Church is outdated and irrelevant. But if we scratch a little under the surface, we see that the Church is extremely relevant in today's world. The world is quick to put a bandage on a wound, so to speak, while the Church tries to address the whole issue before making a decision. The Church takes things slowly, because the Church sees the deep importance of the decisions being made. This perceived slowness can be frustrating to a generation of people who want results yesterday and expect immediate responses from their friends when they text. In a world of instant gratification, waiting is becoming a lost art.

It all matters. If there is one message to share with young Catholics, it's this: It all matters. There are innumerable occasions throughout our day when the Lord is speaking to us and giving us opportunities to grow in holiness. If we see every moment as an opportunity to love God and grow more deeply in relationship with him, then our lives have purpose. When a mother wakes up and changes her baby's diaper or makes her family breakfast with love, she is growing in holiness. It may not be front-page news, but it is the life of an everyday Christian. We shouldn't disdain the everyday tasks put before us. What we may call monotonous or drudgery, God sees as sanctification and holiness.

Through his work with FOCUS and Belmont Abbey College, Tom has seen young men and women answer Christ's call in unique and profound ways. These young men and women have set their eyes on heaven and are accepting nothing less. Tom is always encouraged by how relevant the Catholic faith can be if one is willing to open one's heart just a little. Here is one example he shared:

> My first year at the University of Kentucky as a FOCUS missionary, I met a young man through our outreach toward the beginning of the year. The first time we met, I went with another missionary to his dorm room, and we ended up talking about the *Catechism* for two hours. Fired up about this guy, I was ready to mentor him and get him involved in a Bible study—but he had other plans. Every time I would invite him to a Bible study or just to hang out, he would stand me up. I would go to an agreed-upon place to meet him, and he wouldn't show. By the grace of God, I was able to be patient. Eventually I saw this young man grow into a relational evangelizer with a sincere heart for the New Evangelization and prayer. He left after his second year at Kentucky and entered the seminary. I walked with him through many tough decisions and trials, and what I saw was the light of Christ shining through this young man in a way I had never seen before. He is such an inspiration to me and a sincere brother.

With all of the things Tom is doing to help young people grow in their faith, how does he balance his own faith, family, and work responsibilities? How does he keep things in perspective? He believes that communication is critical at home, and he works hard to make sure he and his wife are on the same page. He has learned the hard way that life is a marathon and not a sprint. Late-night diaper changes, rocking kids to sleep, and transporting them here and there provide awesome opportunities to be grateful for the gift of life.

Tom contests the popular sentiment that "life is about the journey and not the destination." He knows very well that our destination is heaven, and nothing is more important than getting there. In his prayer life, Tom focuses on keeping it simple. Instead of praying for twenty things, he focuses on one or two and tries to listen as much as possible during prayer. He likes to view his prayer life as a "slow burn" and sees numerous opportunities throughout his busy day to pray. He has a wonderful viewpoint on grace:

> If we truly believe that God is eternal and that his grace is eternal, his blessings from years ago are still working in my life. I can tap into that grace when I need a reminder of his great love for and patience with me. I kind of see it as a "Rolodex" of grace. I try not to fit God into my life but rather fit myself into the life God has all around me. There is plenty of grace for my sanctification in every moment of every day.

• THREE WAYS TO HELP YOUNG ADULTS KEEP THEIR CATHOLIC FAITH ALIVE •

You may be thinking that this chapter does not apply to you because you are not a young adult, or you have young children or no children at all. Please think again. Helping young people is everyone's responsibility. They are the future of the Church, and they need our help. Here are three key lessons to draw from Tom MacAlester's story and example:

Be willing to trust in God and make a leap of faith. As Tom's story illustrates, we don't always know exactly what God has in mind for us, but we don't need to be paralyzed by fear and thus do nothing. We might choose to volunteer more at our parish, perhaps getting involved with the teen programs. We can contact local college Catholic student centers for volunteer opportunities. Consider joining together with others in your parish community and reaching out to former local Catholic high school students who are now in college. Invite them to Mass or out for a cup of coffee to start a dialogue.

Model the Catholic faith everywhere. No matter what our age, gender, or family status, we all have a duty to authentically live out our Catholic faith. One of the best ways we can make Christ and the Church more attractive is to truly live what we believe and be the light of Christ to others. We will have a better chance of keeping our young adults in the Church if they see the generations ahead of them boldly pursuing sainthood!

Give kids a great example to follow. This lesson is specifically for parents with children not yet in college. Every study I have seen says that children are highly likely to model the faith habits of their parents. It is difficult to acknowledge, but are we doing our best at home with our kids? We should be leading the family in prayer each night and before all meals. We can form the habit of praying the rosary with our family and going to Eucharistic Adoration with them. Think of the benefits to our children if they see Mom and Dad on their knees in prayer. When we are excited about going to Mass, we'll be an encouragement to our children, making sure they know the gift they have been given as Catholics in the Eucharist.

• QUESTIONS FOR REFLECTION •

1: What has been my attitude toward the Catholic young people I have encountered in my parish community and elsewhere? How have I tried to engage and help them? If I've been indifferent toward them, what can I do to change this?

2: Do I model an authentic Catholic faith at home with my family? If my children are destined to model my faith when they are adults, will that be a good thing?

3: Am I too focused on the day-to-day journey of my life? Or do I keep my eyes on heaven and what I must do to get me, my family, and everyone else there? What would my life be like if this became my focus, and how would it affect those around me?

4: Do I recognize how much God truly loves me? How does this understanding of the heavenly Father's love play out in my life and in how I practice my Catholic faith?

CHAPTER NINE

Sharing Our God-Given Talents

• CONTRIBUTING TO PARISH AND MINISTRY LIFE •

~~~

As each one has received a gift, employ it for one another, as
good stewards of God's varied grace.

—1 Peter 4:10

~~~

I HAVE ALWAYS HELD GREAT RESPECT FOR THOSE WHO DO MUCH OF THE
work that makes our parishes and Catholic ministries run smoothly.
The old 80/20 rule absolutely applies to the parishes I know, with
20 percent of the parishioners (or less) doing the vast majority of
the work. What I have always appreciated is that most of these good
people don't seem to mind. They see it as their duty and as a way to
serve God and the parish community. I am not aware of any priests
who would not agree on the importance of the contributions these
faithful few make in assisting with the vital work that must be done.
One such person is Judy O'Brien.

Judy is a wife, mother, grandmother, and great-grandmother, with
the energy and passion of a twenty-five-year-old. She is one of the
bedrocks of my parish community, and I have a deep appreciation
for her contributions to several ministries, her clear devotion to the
Church, and her Christ-inspired joy.

Judy, a native of Niagara Falls, New York, is a lifelong Catholic who grew up with a twin sister and three brothers. From an early age, she found hard work and a devotion to the Catholic faith modeled by her parents. Their example formed her character and inspired how Judy lives out her faith today. She shared this insight:

> I love my Church and all the opportunities it gives me to serve the Lord and others. I know that my parents were a great influence on me. I saw them both sacrifice everything for our family. My father worked three jobs at times, and my mom worked tirelessly at home for us. She managed to care for elderly and ill neighbors while raising our large family. Because of my parents' example of hard work and love, I have always understood that I should also share that love with others, and I have tried to do that all my life. My husband has attended daily Mass for all our married life, which I had not done until we moved to the South. His devotion to daily Mass led me to follow his example, and I am convinced that receiving the Eucharist daily has a lot to do with my becoming an active member of our parish.

Judy finds that pro-life ministry is the most challenging and rewarding ministry for her. She devotes much of her time to praying at abortion mills for an end to abortion and fund-raising to save babies and mothers from this evil. She participates in Eucharist Adoration twice a week, which keeps her focused on the love of Jesus and energizes her to help others who are in need. She attends a Marian Cenacle led weekly by a priest, where the participants honor Our Lady by consecrating themselves to her, praying the rosary, and reading meditations from one of the Marian Movement of Priests books. Judy says that being involved in the life of the parish has enriched her life more than she could have ever imagined and given her an amazing support group of faith-filled women who inspire her daily.

I asked Judy her thoughts on why many Catholics do not participate more fully in parish life:

> I think some Catholics are lukewarm and lazy in their faith and too involved in secular activities, so they don't have time for their spiritual life. I would encourage them to receive the sacraments more often—especially receiving the Eucharist and going to reconciliation. This would increase their faith. Surely this would help them to share their God-given talents with others.

Seeking other voices to complement Judy's example, I reached out to a Catholic man living in Washington, D.C., named Christian Moran. Christian grew up in Greensboro, North Carolina, the youngest of four children. He described his Catholic upbringing as "quite ordinary." His family went to Mass every Sunday, and every night the children knelt around their parents' bed to pray an Our Father, Hail Mary, and a memorized personal family prayer. Dinnertime always began with an unscripted grace over meals. Even though they had these solid habits, Christian says that religion was rarely discussed in their home.

> Growing up, I didn't have the first clue about church or religion, and I wasn't particularly curious. I was public-schooled, so I never had any religion classes for which I actually felt responsible. My CCD classes left me with nothing memorable at all. I don't know if it was because the instructors were uninspired, or I was uninspired, or both. But nothing

registered. I was bored at Mass, and I would do anything to skip CCD. Only God knows how I got confirmed—I have almost no memory of it. But at some point after that, around the age of fifteen, I do remember saying to myself, "Well, look, either I've got to stop going to Mass, or I can try and get into it, but I can't go on like this." Since I knew I couldn't stop going to Mass as long as I was living under my parents' roof, it occurred to me that one thing I could do to educate myself about the Mass would be to read the Bible. They seemed to read a lot from that book during the Mass, so why not read it myself?

This began a journey through the Gospels for Christian, who was utterly fascinated by what he read. It was the beginning of what would change everything for him.

I will never forget those first few hours after I began reading! It was a study Bible, and the words of Jesus were in red, with the narrative in black. I was almost immediately enthralled. Words cannot express what came over me in the reading of that Gospel—chapter after chapter, every night for the next several weeks—except utter shock, amazement, and indescribable love and joy. That experience over those several weeks was one of truly meeting Jesus Christ, of whom I had been totally ignorant. Since then I've never experienced any troubling doubts about his true identity as God.

Christian's father introduced him to the life and works of John Henry Cardinal Newman. Christian says that Newman's life and his writings were a little more academic than he was really prepared to absorb at the time, especially with no exposure to adequate catechesis. He did take notice of the persecution Newman experienced in his day when he converted to Catholicism from the Anglican Church.

> Newman's example would serve as a kind of shield in college, where nondenominational Christian fellowship groups made it possible for many of my friends to abandon the Catholic Church. I chose instead to dig deeper into the Catholic faith, even though in retrospect I didn't understand it fully, and Newman's example went a long way toward my seeking greater understanding. I'm grateful to both my mom and dad, because in different ways they made it possible for me to perceive the Catholic faith, even though I only became aware of its richness after I had left home.

After earning his undergraduate degree from the University of North Carolina at Chapel Hill in 1994, Christian worked for six months as a residential counselor at a Catholic orphanage and school for abused children called Village of St. Joseph. He began a career as a commercial lender for Bank of America in Atlanta, and he stayed busy as a volunteer youth leader at Christ the King Cathedral. The fire for his Catholic faith only grew stronger as the years went on, and Christian became more and more passionate about serving others.

In 1998, Christian moved to Baltimore to do mission work with the Capuchin Franciscan Volunteer Corps. The program consists of a full year of volunteer service, living in the inner city to serve the poor and residing in a faith community with other lay volunteers. Upon completion of his work with the Capuchins, he moved to Philadelphia, where he received an MBA from the Wharton School of Business at the University of Pennsylvania. Then he moved to Washington, D.C., to begin a career in real estate finance. In 2005, he founded his own real estate investment business called Luminous Properties, which seeks to promote economic justice through the filter of Catholic social teaching.

As I have gotten to know Christian, I have found his obvious humility and awareness of his limitations refreshing. He strives to do great things for Christ and the Church but prays constantly for help with his shortcomings. He says:

> When it comes to humility, one of my favorite saints is St. Francis. There was apparently one occasion when one of his followers praised him for his humility. Francis's answer was to retort that anyone else who'd been given as much grace and as many gifts from God as he had received would have been able to do far more. I've always appreciated this radical perspective of Francis, because he reframed everything about himself that others observed and recognized the real Judge. He knew that the judgment of human beings is, in a sense, relative to God's gifts and expectations of us, not to whatever expectations human beings might have. Unfortunately, I most certainly am guilty of being concerned with worldly opinions, the fear of humiliation, the desire for approval, the desire to go along, and the tendency to grade myself on a curve relative to others. And in the end, this is of course pharisaical, because the Pharisees were concerned with being seen as good while actually doing relatively little in the eyes of God. So let me confess right up front, I have something in common with the Pharisees, so may God help me!
>
> Part of my challenge has been to figure out how to serve the Lord in ways that avoid my particular weaknesses or temptations, while at least trying to fulfill the particular

strengths that I believe he has given me. For this reason, it has always been simpler for me to try to live out my calling as a Catholic in ways that are very ordinary, even mundane from the perspective of a Washingtonian.

One of Christian's favorite ministries is RCIA (the Rite of Christian Initiation for Adults). Partly because of his own lack of catechesis as a young man, and partly because he is inspired by the energy and love of the faith adults often have when seeking to join the Catholic Church, he is drawn to the work of adult faith formation. He relishes his role as someone who can help stir the fire that already exists in their hearts:

> Having grown up in the Protestant South, and having bene-
> fitted from the biblical enthusiasm of Protestantism but
> grown weary of the errors of Protestant theology, I am deeply
> committed to helping my local parish's RCIA program. In
> each class, there are typically Protestants who have various
> levels of understanding about Catholicism and usually a
> fair number of misconceptions. I've always felt that, as a lay
> Catholic, I bring something to the RCIA candidates and
> catechumens that a priest doesn't bring: the simple example
> of an ordinary Catholic. Explaining the Church's teachings
> from the perspective of a layman might show that our faith is
> not something that only the priests and the hierarchy under-
> stand—that yes, Catholics in the pew can read their Bible
> every day, understand and defend the Church's doctrine, and
> love this Church too!

Christian is involved in other ministries, one of which is called Christopolis, founded by a Scottish priest named Peter Magee.

Young adults, both married and single, gather monthly in somebody's home for dinner and a talk, usually based on a reading related to the Church's teaching on a current event or topic. They follow this with an interactive discussion and communal prayer. The mission of the group is to help bring Christ to the city (hence the name Christopolis). The participants in the group seek not only to make a difference in the public square and defend the Church's teachings in the modern world but also to better form themselves in the teachings of Christ and his Church. The group has formed a wonderful partnership with the brothers and priests at the nearby Dominican House of Studies, who have become the generous backbone of the Christopolis mission.

Christian also cofounded a men's group a few years ago. They jokingly call themselves the "Virtuosos," because they want to become more virtuous men. Their evening meeting typically consists of a homemade dinner, a spiritual program, and prayer, but the men will often just discuss topical issues. They sometimes attend Mass together or watch a video series as part of their meeting, such as Father Robert Barron's *Catholicism* series. They hold each other accountable on ways to grow in their spiritual lives. Christian has found that asking for prayer intentions is also a wonderful way to get prayers answered and learn what's going on with each of the men in attendance. The key is to create a trusting atmosphere for men, where they can have fellowship and grow in their faith together. He provided this insight into one of the reasons these groups are so important:

> I started the group because it seems pretty obvious that male friendship and males in general are in a state of crisis. Young adult males today feel isolated, don't have strong male bonds with each other, and perhaps due to our individualistic

culture, seem to want to pretend that they don't need friends. But in fact, we know that "faithful friends are a sturdy shelter" (Sirach 6:14), and it is particularly true among men that "iron sharpens iron" (Proverbs 27:17). Therefore men need each other for fellowship, accountability, and the cultivation of virtue. Even if a man has a girlfriend or wife, he can still feel lonely and isolated and in need of male support. Yet all of this goes unrecognized.

There is one more investment Christian makes in others that I found very convicting: He goes out of his way to befriend priests who cross his path. Think about it. How often do we look at our priests as simply the dispensers of the Eucharist at Mass or those we visit in the confessional? Priests lead a stressful and often isolated existence. They are here to be our shepherds, but they need (and deserve) our support and our friendship. Christian says:

> Priests are good souls, and you really can't ask for a better friend than a priest. But to be sure, it can take initiative to be a friend to a priest, because priests obviously live in a different social universe from married and single people, and they can feel a bit cut off from the rest of the world. They need friends who are not other priests. One priest told me over dinner some time ago that he deeply appreciated my friendship, and it reassured him that he was not "crazy" for getting up in front of people day after day and talking about Jesus. It dawned on me then that priests can feel the strangeness of their vocation in a world that talks incessantly about things of little consequence but very little about the things of God. Another priest told me that many years ago, priests

were much more woven into the lives of their congregation, perhaps being on call to go to a house and resolve a dispute, for example, or just go visit a person who was feeling troubled. Now, with the rising individualism and secularism in our society, we can sometimes make our priests feel as if they are just a handshake at the end of Mass. But priests in so many ways are just like the rest of us, in need of friendship and fellowship. I hope to be lucky enough to count more priests as good friends in the years to come.

Some of us may not feel we are blessed with Christian Moran's God-given ability to organize, lead, encourage, and make a significant difference in the lives of many people, but consider these insights gleaned from his example, and be encouraged to make a difference.

Understand the importance of self-awareness. We all fall short in various areas and in various degrees. Self-awareness helps us know where we need to grow and where we need help. Where can we apply our faith next? Where will investing in our faith reap the greatest returns? We need self-awareness in order to fulfill our calling in Christ.

Be willing to give and share first. If we want others to be transparent with us, we must be willing to be transparent first. If we are leading a Bible study, for instance, and want to solicit a response from the participants, we might reveal our insights first. Our focus should always be on giving, and a good motto might be "Give first!" Our attitude toward giving has a lot to do with how people respond to us.

Be authentic. When we're real about who we are, honest about our own shortcomings, others will be more likely to risk being real with us. Another aspect of authenticity is letting our true light shine:

not being afraid to let the world see our peace and joy but having the freedom to be ourselves, weaknesses and all.

• FOUR WAYS TO CONTRIBUTE TO PARISH AND MINISTRY LIFE •
Judy O'Brien and Christian Moran are committed to giving their God-given talents to the Church, to parish ministries, and to others in need. They love Christ and the Church, and their joyful witness is a beacon of light to anyone fortunate enough to encounter them. There are four important actions we can draw from how they live their lives to help others:

Receive the Eucharist daily and attend Eucharistic Adoration. Judy O'Brien credits her husband's example of attending daily Mass as the catalyst that drew her into a more active life at her parish. We will act more as Jesus does in serving others if we take him into our bodies each day and pray before the true presence in Eucharistic Adoration.

Be humble. Both Judy and Christian possess great humility and would rather talk about anything but their work. By detaching ourselves from "who gets the credit," we have more freedom to serve and can focus on giving the glory to God.

See a need? Get something started. Christian's example with his men's group is a great illustration of seeing a problem (lack of fellowship and accountability among Catholic men) and doing something proactive and fun to address the need. We all have opportunities to take initiative this way—we don't need to wait for permission!

Keep it simple. In their own individual ways, Judy and Christian focus on simple ways to make a difference: pray for an end to abortions, attend daily Mass, have dinner and Bible study with friends, befriend priests, and so on. Making a difference in your parish and community doesn't require an elaborate plan. It only requires you.

• Questions for Reflection •

1: Am I using my God-given talents to serve others? What is preventing me? Can I identify the obstacles and overcome them?

2: Am I part of the 20 percent of people in my parish the author described at the beginning of the chapter? Do I pull my weight and do my share? How can I get more involved, starting immediately?

3: Christian is a great example of someone who overcame the poor catechesis of his young years, learned about our Catholic faith as he got older, and became actively engaged in the practice of our faith. Am I properly formed as a Catholic? If not, what can I do about it?

4: Do I recognize how important the sacramental life of the Church is in the practice of my faith? Do I go to reconciliation frequently and attend Mass as often as possible, not just on Sundays?

CHAPTER TEN

An Unlikely Hero

• PASSING ON THE CATHOLIC FAITH TO OUR CHILDREN •

~~~

Education in the faith by the parents should begin in the child's earliest years. This already happens when family members help one another to grow in faith by the witness of a Christian life in keeping with the Gospel. Family catechesis precedes, accompanies, and enriches other forms of instruction in the faith. Parents have the mission of teaching their children to pray and to discover their vocation as children of God. The parish is the Eucharistic community and the heart of the liturgical life of Christian families; it is a privileged place for the catechesis of children and parents.

—*CCC* 2226, citing *Lumen Gentium*, 11

~~~

KEN DAVISON AND HIS WIFE, KERRI, HAVE EIGHT BEAUTIFUL CHILDREN. I have enjoyed my friendship with Ken, a man who truly feels blessed by his family and grateful for every minute he spends with them. As I was praying about which Catholics to write about in *Joyful Witness*, I inexplicably felt that I should write about Kerri Davison, not Ken. I was intrigued by the incredible job she has done not only as a homeschooling mother of eight thriving children but also as a driving force behind Holy Heroes, the family business she runs with Ken.

Holy Heroes was started in 2007 by the Davisons, and they run it with the active involvement of their children. The goal of the business is to "bring the joy of the faith" to other families, and they accomplish this by producing books, CDs, and videos. Kerri told me that they regularly hear from families telling them how much they have learned from Holy Heroes. Other times Kerri and Ken hear that it is the *Davison children* teaching *other children* that makes what they provide so mesmerizing. As Kerri shared with me:

> There is so much garbage in our culture trying to distort and captivate the imaginations of our children; our goal is to capture their imaginations for Christ. Many people want to know about their faith, but they were never taught it and do not even know where to begin in teaching their children. We want to help. It is hard to focus on what really matters. There is so much to distract us in the world from our ultimate goal: heaven. Getting ourselves and our families (and anyone else we can help) to heaven is the only thing that ultimately matters.

You might think Kerri's story is all about her large family and their exciting business, but you would only be partially correct. What makes Kerri Davison's story fascinating is the long and hard-fought faith journey that brought her to this place in her life. She has given her own children and countless thousands of families through Holy Heroes the Catholic education experience she never had for herself. As she explains:

> I'm from New York City. I was raised in a culturally Catholic family, but with no real understanding of the faith. When we were little children, my mother always took us to Sunday Mass, and we received the sacraments, but we were never

taught about the faith nor how to live as a Catholic. (The CCD classes we attended unfortunately covered neither.) We never prayed as a family. I saw the Catholic faith simply as a collection of meaningless rituals. As I grew older, I was only too happy to cast it off. However, even though I did not know what I was leaving, I acutely felt the lack of God in my life and spent a great deal of time and energy trying to find what was missing over the ensuing years.

Kerri met Ken, a Methodist from the Midwest, while they were both in graduate school overseas. Ken no longer practiced his Protestant faith when they met, but he had a continued interest in God, which Kerri found very attractive. Kerri says they both felt a longing for God and were intellectually curious about religion.

We loved each other and wanted to get married before Ken's military assignments would separate us geographically. I also wanted our love blessed by God with a marriage in a church, not just codified by the government in some sort of civil ceremony. This posed a difficulty, because we had no place to get married (we weren't members of any church or parish), and there was no one to marry us. After much distress over our situation, it turned out that the fastest and easiest way for us to marry was in a Catholic church at West Point, because Ken had graduated from the Air Force Academy. By the grace of God (and some military academy reciprocity!), we ended up married within three months of our engagement, in a Catholic church. Looking back, I can see that God arranged our wedding in a Catholic church, though at the time I never thought of this.

Kerri and Ken were married for five years before their first child was born. Kerri says that during those years they discussed religion, often heatedly.

> Ken's search took him far away from Christianity into Eastern mysticism, where he could intellectually think about God but not have it affect the way he intended to live his life. My interest in religion was more practical: I was interested in how to raise our children. When we got married in a Catholic church, we chafed a bit at the promise we had to make to raise our children Catholic, but at the time I couldn't foresee that this would entail very much difficulty. After all, I had been raised Catholic.
>
> Now that we had a child, it was time to follow through. We had our first daughter baptized and, while doing so, tried to discover what baptism meant—with no success. Perhaps I was too busy to take the time to understand, but it seemed to me that there was no one in the couple of Catholic churches that I went to who understood what baptism *was*. I was told at one church that baptism is "an initiation into a club." The whole experience left me unsatisfied.

After a move to another state, they met and became friends with a group of evangelical Baptist neighbors. Kerri and Ken started reading the Bible and attending Bible studies. Ken was intellectually interested in what he was learning, and once he understood who Jesus was and really began to know him, he became an intellectually convinced Christian. He no longer had any interest in Eastern religions. This was a relief to Kerri, who never had any attraction to religions besides Christianity.

Kerri began to think the easiest way for them to be Christians would be to become Protestant, especially since Ken's family was Protestant. But she had doubts about their newfound faith in the back of her mind. As she recalls:

The "once saved, always saved" Protestant idea and the idea that God did not expect me to alter my behavior in any way did not resonate with my New Yorker mindset. Even the Our Father prayer told me that I must forgive others in order to be forgiven myself.

At a Protestant Bible study we attended, some things were taught that disturbed both of us and raised questions in our minds. While watching some videos about the Holy Land, for instance, we noticed that there was no mention of any of the ancient churches in the Holy Land, those that had been built over the sites where Jesus was born or crucified. We felt that we were being misinformed and that there was an attempt to conceal things about Christianity that didn't fit into the Protestant framework.

I felt uncomfortable enough with these historical inconsistencies that one day I went into a Catholic bookstore. I asked the owner what book I could read that would explain the difference between Catholicism and Protestantism. She showed me a wall of books (some quite thick). I bought *Born Fundamentalist, Born Again Catholic* by David Currie, and I read it that afternoon. Then I hired a babysitter so I could read every relevant part out loud to Ken over dinner.

We were grateful to our Protestant friends who had taught us enough that, when we heard the truths of the Catholic faith so simply and beautifully explained in that short book, we were changed forever. A friend who had a similar experience later told me it was like being "sucked out of an airplane" after a window had broken open in flight. So it was for us. We were immediately and irresistibly pulled into the Catholic Church. I believe that over the next years we became one of that Catholic bookstore's best customers!

After Kerri and Ken became practicing Catholics, they became aware of how easy it is to grow up Catholic while never learning anything about Catholicism. Kerri shared this life-changing moment:

Once while browsing in the Catholic bookstore, I read something in a children's catechism. The answer to the question "Why did God make you?" was "God made me to show his goodness and to make me happy with him in heaven." What? The answer to the question that plagues most of humanity is here on page 9 of a children's catechism! How can it be that my husband and I had never heard such a simple answer? With all of our education, we would not have been able to answer this fundamental question. What an amazing gift this kind of knowledge is for us. We did not want our children to grow up without it.

After researching the school choices near their home, both public and Catholic, the Davisons decided to follow the example of some good friends and homeschool their children. Sixteen years later they are still at it! Kerri believes that homeschooling answered the problem of how to pass on the faith to their children while providing them with a good education. Their homeschooling experience has evolved into their work of passing on the Catholic faith through Holy Heroes.

How does this busy mother of eight, devoted wife, homeschooling mom, and active businesswoman possibly get everything done each day? Here is solid advice we can follow from Kerri's life:

Getting anything done just takes a lot of work. There's no secret to getting everything done—getting anything done takes a lot of work. And it's good to remember that everything does *not* always get done. However, with hard work, whatever is important does get done.

Choose the most important things. There's always a tendency to neglect the most important things because lesser things seem more appealing. It takes discipline to focus on what's most important and not let distractions interfere. If there is extra time and energy, that can be used to do extra things.

Keep a family calendar. "Even if time management is not part of your nature, it's necessary for families, large or small. A family calendar that lists everyone's commitments and appointments, combined with a daily schedule that shows what the kids have to accomplish during the day, will keep everyone on track. Schoolwork, chores, extracurricular activities, and work commitments all go on the calendar. No schedule will always work smoothly—it's a work in progress."

Make regular prayer an integral part of life. Schedule family prayer time so it becomes an integral part of your life. Get in the habit of saying prayers before and after each meal. Say a morning offering together at breakfast, and recite the Angelus at lunch. Say night-time prayers together every night—consider an evening rosary—and encourage your children to pray in their beds before falling asleep. You might keep a book of people and things that your family is praying for. The Davisons pray before they start trips, and they pray at the end of trips. Ken regularly takes the children with him to his weekly Holy Hour. Develop the habit of praying at every opportunity, when something you see or hear reminds you: When an ambulance passes, pray for the sick or injured; when you're passing a cemetery, pray for the dead. Before you know it, regular prayer will be part of your life and your children's lives too!

Doing something is better than doing nothing. Kerri has a little motto: "Something is better than nothing." In other words, doing something is better than doing nothing. For example: You are too tired to say a whole rosary with your children—then say a decade instead. You do not have time to go over an entire catechism lesson— then just have everyone memorize *one* catechism question. If you were to live an entire year like this, you would have said seventy-three rosaries and memorized 365 catechism questions. This idea is the same with housework, schoolwork, and works of charity.

Listen to good advice and follow great examples. Don't be afraid to seek the advice of others who have been in situations similar to yours. They may have valuable wisdom to impart. Friends can share how they have dealt with their own challenges, and our heavenly friends, the saints, will always help us keep things in perspective. We have the great leisure of learning our faith at a time in history when we can learn it and teach it in peace. That will probably not always be the case; we should take full advantage of it.

Kerri's "Best Practices" List for Growing Faith-Filled Children

With all of the incredible experiences in her own life and the stories she hears from families who buy from Holy Heroes, I was keenly interested in learning from Kerri what her "best practices" list would be to help families pass the Catholic faith on to their children.

Recognize the fact that we no longer live in a Christian culture. "It is not just what is missing from families but what is missing from our culture. We no longer live in a Christian culture. This happened slowly over decades, but now with ever increasing speed, our country is shedding every bit of Christian truth. Parents can no longer rely on the culture, the schools, or even the Church religious education program to teach their children the truths of Catholicism; they must rely on themselves and God."

There is much to learn from the Church's rich history and tradition. "Any pious practice you can incorporate into your family, you should. If you are Catholic, there is almost always a reason for a party (patron saints' days, baptismal days, feast days, and so on). Likewise, there is always some piece of history to be learned from the saint on the calendar that day. There is always something inspiring to be gained from the traditions and rituals and practices that have developed over the years to better reveal to us the mind of God behind the seasons and the rhythm of life."

Take any opportunity to pray with and for your children. "If your children know their prayers, no matter what happens, no matter their state of mind, they will always be able to pray. Get them accustomed to praying all the time, privately and publicly, without embarrassment, without fear. I never saw my parents pray, and I was shocked by the first people I saw praying publicly. It should not be that way with our children. They should be so accustomed to speaking to God that it is second nature. Encourage them to speak to Jesus in their hearts whenever possible, whenever they are happy or sad or confused or anxious—anytime. A good practice is to tell them to go over their day with Jesus before they go to sleep."

Talk about Jesus and your faith in reference to everything else in the world. Our faith should have an effect on everything we do. There's a line in the movie *Chariots of Fire*, where one runner explains to his sister that when he runs, he "feels God's pleasure." What a beautiful way to explain what it means to bring your faith into everything you do! We should feel God's pleasure with everything we do and in every place we are. If we do not, we need to change what we are doing or leave where we are.

Our culture and the world are becoming increasingly irrational and dishonest. Show your children that, by understanding the teachings of the Catholic Church, their lives and choices can make sense and bring joy. Help them make sense of the world as a place of spiritual warfare, where God can triumph even when things look terrible and evil seems to be winning the day.

Teach your children to face the world without fear. "This does not mean that they should be imprudent in where they go and what they do or put themselves in near occasions of sin. But we should teach our children not to be afraid of doing difficult things. They shouldn't be afraid to engage those around them who do not agree with them or to do things that will draw criticism from people who are immersed in the perspectives of the secular world. And as parents we must not be afraid to let our children suffer. The world will not always treat them fairly, especially when they are trying to live a faithful Catholic life. When they are treated unfairly, teach them to face the problem and solve it, if possible, or to accept it and offer it up in union with Christ's suffering for the redemption of us all."

Be a good model of the Catholic faith. "Even more than what you tell them, you need to *show* them all of the above by how you live your life. You won't be perfect, but you can ask forgiveness, go to confession, take a break to pray, and approach life not with anxiety and trepidation but with joy and hope. For heaven is for those who persevere, with God's grace, to the end, in the circumstances Our Father provides us, in every minute on earth, to grow in love for him and each other."

• Three Ways to Pass on the Catholic Faith to Our Children •

Kerri's walk of faith is fascinating when you consider where she began and the great ministry work she is doing today for Christ, the Church, and our children. Here are three important lessons in her experiences:

Complete trust in God will be rewarded. Kerri and Ken Davison have built their lives (and committed their future) around the unwavering principle of trust in God. We can also do great things for God if we are willing to shed the nagging doubts that plague most of us and detach from the illusory promises of the secular world.

We must rely on God and our own efforts. We no longer live in a Christian culture. The world, schools, and even parish-based faith programs will not adequately teach the Catholic faith to our children. It is *our* responsibility. We have an opportunity to take charge of our children's faith education and ensure that they know and live their Catholic faith and are well prepared for a journey that will lead them to heaven.

Integrate the practice of our Catholic faith into everything we do. Start small, but get started immediately with some of the best practices Kerri offered earlier in the chapter. Make sure you have no "silos" where you store your faith, but bring your faith with you everywhere you go, especially into your home. Don't practice the Catholic faith only in Mass on Sunday.

• Questions for Reflection •

1: How am I a role model for my children when it comes to the practice of my Catholic faith? Can I teach them what I don't know? If I am lacking in confidence and knowledge, am I willing to learn with them?

2: Have I relinquished the faith education of my children to schools and parish religious programs, or do I clearly see that this is my responsibility? What am I doing to supplement what my children are learning about their faith from other sources?

3: How would I describe my vocation as a parent (or future parent)? What am I doing to help those around me, especially my children, get to heaven?

4: How can I teach my children or other young people to understand the world and live in it without fear? What practical ideas can I begin to implement this week?

CHAPTER ELEVEN

Life in the Fast Lane

· SECOND CHANCES AND APPLYING
THE CATHOLIC FAITH TO BUSINESS ·

~~~

This split between the faith which many profess and their daily lives deserves to be counted among the more serious errors of our age.

—Gaudium et Spes, 43

~~~

I WAS SIGNING BOOKS ON THE SECOND EVENING OF THE 2013 CATHOLIC Marketing Network Trade Show in New Jersey when a tall man in a suit stood in front of me and said, "Hello, Randy, I'm Andy LaVallee." I had exchanged e-mails with Andy a few times over the years, after contacting him about his work with the Massachusetts Catholic Business Conference. I had heard great things about the way Andy ran his company, LaVallee's Bakery Distributors, from a Catholic perspective and was pleased to finally meet him. His energy and obvious passion for the Catholic faith were immediately obvious. In less than five minutes, I knew this man loved Christ and the Church and was committed to serving others. Our brief meeting left a strong impression on me, and Andy was one of the first people I thought to include in *Joyful Witness.*

Andy, a Boston native, has been married to his wife, Barbara, for almost forty years and is partners in his bakery business with his children, Nicole and Jeffrey. He was raised by faithful Catholic parents, the oldest of three boys in the tough streets of Boston's Charlestown neighborhood, where fighting and violence were a way of life. He remembers positive lessons: Work harder than everyone else, be loyal, and trust those who support you.

Andy drifted away from the Church, and he blames himself for having his priorities in the wrong order.

> In 1977, I founded LaVallee's Bakery Distributors by buying a station wagon for four hundred dollars and delivering bread on my way home from my full-time job at Quinzani's Bakery. Building this business drove me to be the best in our industry. My work and the business became the number one thing in my life, and I believed all my success was because of me and no one else.
>
> One business was not enough. While my wife was pregnant with our first child, I founded LaVallee Thoroughbred Racing Stables. Making money drove me. From 1977 to 1982, I won over one hundred races with my stable. But I sensed I was heading toward a big-time disaster if I did not leave this business. I woke up one morning and decided to sell everything and get out.

Things changed slightly when Andy began to go to Mass occasionally on Sunday. His pastor asked him to teach the boys' confirmation class until he could find someone else. Andy went to Mass each week and taught the class, but he was not living the teaching he was sharing with the boys. He shared this painful recollection:

Outside things were great, but inside I was not the man I wanted to be. I was drinking excessively, making excuses for my actions, lying, and really hurting those who loved me. I was living a divided life; I was very insincere, truly prideful, and really phony.

Some people go through an entire life not knowing their purpose or why God has given them the gifts he has. Up until June 2010, I was a secure, self-employed businessman. My priorities were business, golf, friends, family, and God— in that order. I remembered God mostly when I needed him.

Andy met Jim Caviezel, the star of *The Passion of the Christ*, at a Catholic Men's Conference in 2010, and the Catholic movie star invited Andy to go to Medjugorje. At the time, Medjugorje was not on Andy's radar. He remembers telling Jim, "Don't get your hopes up. I am not flying fifteen hours to say a rosary."

But he did go to Medjugorje. For Andy, this trip that he reluctantly took completely changed his life. Here is his experience:

Our Lady has a way of showing us a different path, and she certainly did with me. I am forever grateful for her love and the direction she used to bring me back to her Son. While in Medjugorje for the first time, I experienced what I call a "life confession" behind St. James Church that was full of love, forgiveness, and continuous tears. After two and a half hours, my shirt was soaked. This single experience of the sacrament of reconciliation has made the biggest impact on my life. Confession is one of the sacraments many of us seldom take advantage of. I am now a daily Mass participant and a daily Scripture reader. I pray the rosary daily, go to confession weekly, and have begun fasting regularly. The profound intercession of Our Lady, along with returning to the sacraments, has transformed my life, and I am extremely grateful to her.

Profound Business Changes

Once Andy experienced this reversion, it was important to him to live it in all phases of his life. He made a new set of priorities, with God first, and began studying the Catholic faith in earnest. He was especially interested in learning more about the virtues and Catholic social doctrine and how these can be applied to business. Andy began following a set of core principles in his business life that are in alignment with the teachings of the Catholic Church.

Be a good steward. "First and foremost, for me it was really important to start looking at my business as a gift from God. Being the steward of this gift was not about financial statements or the bottom line but about my answer at Judgment Day when asked by the Creator what I did with this gift."

Be a servant leader. The second cornerstone principle of Andy's business is servant leadership. We need to take the real life lessons of Jesus; he served everyone around him. Think of the feeding of the five thousand and the multiplication of the five loaves and two fish. We too can follow Jesus's example and learn to lead as he did.

Follow Catholic social doctrine. Catholic social doctrine includes four core ethics that show us how to solve dilemmas when they are presented to us as leaders. First, respect the dignity of all people. Second, make decisions for the common good. Third, look to the front line for the people who are closest to the problem. Finally, the result of the first three concepts coming together, build a solid, trustful work environment.

Andy says the game changer that propelled his company to the next level was Pope Benedict's encyclical *Caritas in Veritate* (Charity in Truth). He considers this one of the best business books ever written and thinks it should be a must-read for every businessperson. Andy says:

> Benedict wrote this right after the stock market crash in 2008, and in it he offered solutions for developing the real assets in business: people. The Holy Father was asking us to seek hybrid programs that could develop and help people and business enterprises. This encyclical provided the motivation for my company to transform our biggest department, our distribution program, into something more devout.

LaVallee Bakery Distributors has become a modern-day case study of how stewardship, servant leadership, and Catholic social doctrine work in a very competitive business marketplace. Andy has been blessed with the opportunity to speak about this doctrine and about the true benefits of developing a business based on it. Not only has he addressed a very secular group of over two hundred business leaders, who comprise the Small Business Association of New England (SBANE), but he was also invited by Andreas Widmer to be a guest professor at Catholic University's Entrepreneurial School of Business Ethics.

Andy acknowledges that, even though being a true Catholic businessperson in today's world places him in the minority, he wants everyone to understand that it works. He believes that Catholic business leaders who humbly approach this concept will be able to stimulate the economy and bring the people around them to their full potential for the benefit of all. He encourages leaders to focus on serving others, developing their teams' God-given talents, and making business decisions for the common good.

Andy is aware of the significant level of temptations we face whenever we bring our Catholic faith into our business life. He stresses:

> The Catholic business leader needs to have a disciplined prayer life based around the daily sacraments, most importantly the Holy Eucharist at Mass; this is vital with regard to your business. The Catholic business leader also needs to embrace a high level of virtue and to practice love and forgiveness as keys to living the truth of the Gospel in the workplace. This is where confession comes in. Once you receive the mercy and forgiveness of God, it's hard not to forgive others.

Andy told me a compelling story of the virtue of forgiveness carried out at LaVallee's, a story rarely heard of in business today.

> Our assistant operations manager has been with us for twelve years, ever since his freshman year of high school. He was brought up in a tough environment and has anger issues. After he got in a conflict with his supervisor, I explained to him that I had to write him up with a warning. All he had to do was sign off on the warning. We would put it in his file and work toward improvement. He is like a second son to me, but when the conversation escalated, it turned into my pride against his, and I fired him.
>
> Over the next few hours, in his anger he deleted $25,000 worth of orders. His actions created a very challenging next few days. Off I went to prayer, and the Holy Spirit kept pounding me for an entire week with examples of forgiveness.

I realized that God was asking me to put my pride aside and show forgiveness to this young man. After much prayer and discernment, I composed a memo of forgiveness, so that my entire company would understand the power of this virtue. Then I rehired the young man. My employees were shocked; it looked to them like weakness. But then I turned around a few days later at daily Mass to give the sign of peace, and there he was, back at Holy Mass and the sacraments for the first time since his confirmation. That moment showed me that I did the right thing, and the rest is up to God.

Being bold about one's faith is part of the LaVallee culture, with positive results:

The leader needs to lead with love in order to empower others. Effective leaders recognize it's not about them—it's about developing the talents of those around them. Part of leading with love is being true to one's faith without fear.

Once we had a meeting with one of our vendors who was due to arrive at our office at 9:30 am. He finally showed up at 11:00 am. This was an important company-wide meeting that represented about $300,000 in business. I regularly attend Mass at noon during the week, and when I got up and announced that I was leaving to attend Mass, I turned a few heads. The tough part was leaving everything back at the office while I went to Mass. When I returned an hour later, everything had been resolved. God was in charge and not me.

Andy believes it is important to go from values to virtues. Values are *consciously* executed, while virtues are *subconsciously* executed. Most companies have a "values statement," but very few have a "virtues statement." Being a Catholic business leader assumes a high level of risk. Andy says, "When we have important decisions to make, we reduce the risk factor by going to Our Lord in Eucharistic Adoration. Sit in silence and listen to the path he wants you to take. Invoke the power of the Holy Spirit. There is really no better way."

A Case Study of Success

In order to solve some long-standing problems with his drivers, Andy created a new program based on Pope Benedict's call in the encyclical.

> Our third-shift drivers' responsibility is to deliver our bakery products to all our customers. They must drive the trucks safely, are responsible for the security of keys and alarm codes for certain locations, and engage customers on a day-to-day basis. They were doing all this for a compensation of fourteen to sixteen dollars per hour. This created a revolving door of drivers with the attitude of "I'm just a driver, and if you have a problem, call the office." There was no ownership or stewardship in the job.
>
> Pope Benedict's encyclical inspired us to create a program that would improve and deal with these major issues. He talks about an effective shift in mentality that can lead to the adoption of new lifestyles. This is exactly what happened. We first changed the job title from "driver" to "guardian," and then we trained, taught, and encouraged the concept of servant leadership. This—along with a whole new compensation package based on the efficiency of the deliveries and the growth of each and every bakery route—provided an economic and ethical win for both the company and

the employees. Employees' families and lifestyles changed dramatically from the success of this program. Our business also grew significantly. We called our new program the LaVallee Bakery Guardian program.

If we analyze the program in terms of business metrics and measurable results, the change in practices has first and foremost given Andy's company consecutive years of double-digit growth. Why is this happening in a tough economy? Andy says it is because his company is embracing the most important asset in business: *people.* These virtues and concepts have made Andy's enterprise an example of how a Catholic business can affect many areas of life if leaders are not afraid to truly live out the Gospel and model the faith for all to see.

Live the Fast

During Andy's reconversion, fasting was an accelerator for him to come closer to God. He read books about fasting, and as he researched the practice, he found it was very difficult to practice a bread-and-water fast. Here is what Andy and his company discovered:

> A vast majority of manufacturers use genetically modified flour. This, along with preservatives and additives, makes it almost impossible to engage in a bread-and-water fast. The chemicals you put into your body cause side effects like increased appetite and headaches. We believed we could do something about this. So we decided to launch a pilot program to test our recipe for new fasting breads. The testimonials were amazing, and this gave us an enormous reason to create an ongoing ministry.
>
> As I was praying about the possibility of a year-round fasting program, I asked our Lord to give me a direct message

that I could understand. That same night I received a phone call from my dad's best friend, a man I had not spoken to or seen in over thirty-five years. He had seen an article on LaVallee Fasting Breads in the *Boston Pilot* newspaper, and he called me to say, "I want you to know that if your dad were alive today, he would be very proud of this project. More importantly, I want you to know that you need to continue this: The Church needs fasting."

What would you have done? I cried like a baby, prayed a rosary of thanksgiving, and decided to join the fight to promote fasting, just as Jesus, Mary, and the apostles practiced it over two thousand years ago. The result was the creation of Live the Fast, whose mission is to encourage the practice of prayer and fasting by providing a variety of exceptional, all-natural, nutritious breads, along with educational resources and a support community that will inspire one to fast.

Reflecting on the Last Ten Years

When someone turns his or her life around the way Andy did, that person's family and friends are bound to be impacted. I asked Andy to describe the differences in his lifestyle, and I was curious about the way his friends and family perceived him now versus ten years ago. Andy credits much of where he is today to his wife's love, trust, and loyalty and to the fact that she stuck by him during every twist and turn of his journey. He shared some key reflections on his life then and now:

With a sense of regret, I can remember just a few years ago how filthy my mouth was. I would swear a hundred times per day, lose my patience, and blame others for my weakness. Then, when my conversion came, God stripped all my vices away. He began to show me a better version of myself. It was all his doing, and I am here to say with total confidence that God can do an awful lot with a simple yes.

One of the best fruits of this walk is that my adult children and partners, Jeffrey and Nicole, understand the responsibility of this legacy. We are a faith-filled Catholic business watched over by our Lord and his mother. They plan to carry this on, even in challenging times. We have learned many lessons together as father, son, daughter, and business leaders.

I have lost many old friends with whom I previously spent hours drinking pints and conversing. They just do not understand how different I've become. New acquaintances shake their heads, but deep down I can sense that they want the same peace and trust in God I have.

I would hope my friends and family members would say that they see me now as a more humble and patient leader who puts God first in all things—someone who has his priorities in line and is committed to reaching his full potential. And looking back, all the struggles and suffering, all the joy and happiness, are far more pleasurable when you share them with God!

• Four Ways to Make the Most of Second Chances and Apply the Catholic Faith to Business •

Andy LaVallee has led an incredible life blessed with a strong marriage, wonderful children, and a successful business. But it wasn't until he experienced a powerful reversion to Catholicism and applied his newfound faith to every area of his life, especially his business, that he truly began to live abundantly. Here are four ways we can follow Andy's example:

Value people as your greatest asset. If we are in business and have any leadership responsibility, it is our duty to place the well-being of the people around us ahead of profits. Respect the dignity of all persons.

Daily Mass, sacraments, and prayer. As we have seen from many of the people profiled in *Joyful Witness*, those who attend daily Mass, participate in the sacraments, and have active prayer lives thrive spiritually. We must identify and eliminate any obstacles that stand between us and these practices if we wish to grow in our Catholic faith.

Spend time with those you love. Most of us spend a huge amount of time at work. We also find ample time to watch TV and surf the Internet. Let's make sure we have our priorities straight—with Jesus, family, and work, in that order. If we love Jesus, we must spend quality time with him. Eliminate excuses and ask yourself what is really important.

Commit to becoming a better version of yourself. There is likely a better version of us waiting to emerge, and God is ready and willing to help us make the change. God expected great things of Andy and got his attention. He expects great things from each of us as well. Now is the time to be the Catholic you are called to be.

• QUESTIONS FOR REFLECTION •

1: Have I practiced fasting the way Andy LaVallee has done? Can I see the fruits of fasting, and am I willing to commit to a life that includes fasting and prayer?

2: Do I compartmentalize my life, or do I fully integrate my Catholic faith into all areas of my life, including my work? What are some examples of both?

3: It is clear that God placed people and events in Andy's life on several occasions to get his attention. When have I been aware of the movement of the Holy Spirit in my life, and what was God trying to tell me? How would I describe the movement of the Holy Spirit in my circumstances today?

4: What great things do I sense the Lord has in store for me? Am I ready to be the Catholic I'm meant to be? What would a "better version" of myself actually look like?

CHAPTER TWELVE

Seeking the New Counterculture
· An Authentic and Candid Voice in the World ·

~~~

The duty of Christians to take part in the life of the Church impels them to act *as witnesses of the Gospel* and of the obligations that flow from it. This witness is a transmission of the faith in words and deeds. Witness is an act of justice that establishes the truth or makes it known.

—*CCC* 2472, citing Matthew 18:16

~~~

Kathryn Lopez, the editor-at-large of *National Review Online* *(NRO)*, is a nationally syndicated columnist whose work has been published in a wide variety of publications, including the *Wall Street Journal, New York Times, First Things, National Catholic Register*, Patheos.com, and *Our Sunday Visitor*. She is a director at Catholic Voices USA and speaks frequently on faith and public life on college campuses, radio, and television.

As I read the daily input from this hardworking journalist on issues important and relevant for all Catholics, I am drawn to her passion for truth. She is zealous about making sure that truth is made available for discerning Catholics everywhere, in contrast to what the mainstream media promote.

Kathryn believes all of us are called to be joyful witnesses and to stand up for our faith. We can no longer afford to be bystanders; a radical surrender to Christ is required of each of us. Kathryn strives to be an authentic and candid Catholic voice in journalism. We spoke about the importance of authenticity and being on the front lines of the culture war:

> I certainly pray to be real. Authenticity is a requirement of anyone claiming to be Christian. When we don't live an integrated Catholic life of prayer and discipleship, we contribute to confusion and hurt and scandal around us, and we help evil flourish. We've simply got to be honest in what we do and say.
>
> The warriors on the front lines—in what is very much a spiritual battle for our minds and our souls—are every mother and father, every aunt and uncle, everyone who sacrifices and suffers to make sure that those who are most especially vulnerable in their lives (whom they have a responsibility for and to) see that there is something better than what is much too often presented as the way to live. The front lines are schools and homes and bars and dorms and streets and hospitals.
>
> In any writing and speaking that I do, I hope to highlight some of the good out there, to let people know they are not alone in seeking the new counterculture: lives of joyful witness to the full freedom that is found in radical surrender to Christ.

Each of us is called to lead an authentic Catholic life, and this calls for courage. There is a clear need for a new "counterculture," as Kathryn describes it, to combat the influence of the secular culture, which so negatively impacts our religious freedom and how we practice our faith.

I often find that talented writers have a mentor or great example to follow. For the sake of readers interested in writing or communicating the truth of our faith in the New Evangelization, I asked Kathryn where her love of writing and reporting comes from:

> I would have never seen writing as a vocational option if I hadn't started reading *National Review* in grade school. William F. Buckley, Jr., was a relentless beacon of good writing and good sense. He surrounded himself with talent. And he was rigorous in his intellectual and spiritual pursuits. When he died, George Weigel called him one of the "top Catholic public intellectuals of the century." I don't think people realized, even at the time, what a forum he gave to Catholic ideas, even critiquing some choices a bishops' conference might make here or there! It's a real blessing to have spent some time with him in my early years at *NR* and have had some of my copy marked up by him!
>
> I'm grateful for the opportunities I have to communicate, and that gratitude increases as the world seems to get less certain and less familiar. People are encouraged, feel challenged, and take action through stories and testimonies, sometimes even when someone repeats herself week after week, trying to point to something good and beautiful.
>
> The Holy Spirit is alive in us, and we have a responsibility to listen clearly and take dictation. This is the call. We are tabernacles and instruments of love, if we are receptive and attentive to discernment.

Kathryn shared a few of the challenges affecting the Church today that keep her up at night:

> So many people are in pain. They don't know that they are not alone. When Pope Francis pleads with us to know God's mercy, when Pope Benedict urges us—with a sense of mandate—to encounter Christ daily, these are manifestations of God's constant pleading with us to enter into union with him; to know the love of the Trinity; to know we are never left alone, never left unaided; and to know that we are loved more than we can ever imagine or even desire. Each one of us *is*. Anyone who knows how hard that can be to even begin to comprehend *must* ache for his brother who doesn't know, who doesn't see.
>
> I worry that our priests don't have the support they need, that we owe them so much more for their sacrificial lives of service: more prayer cover, more gratitude, and more hospitality. The world may not know it, but we are blessed by some dynamic, holy priests. True saints. True fathers. The world knows about the filth. And Mass-attending Catholics can all too often be content to criticize a parish priest on his choice of music or a bishop for not being more politically assertive. Maybe first we should a) pray for them, and b) consider whether we ourselves have courage in the public square. Do we show leadership in truth and love?
>
> Do we pray for priests? Do we think of them? Do we offer to lend a hand, offer our expertise and service? Do we let them know there is a welcoming, grateful community of brothers and sisters around them? Do we help them tell the truth? Do we encourage them when they are courageous?

Or do we whine? Do we take good and holy men for granted and—while knowing they suffer in the wake of the horrific sins, mistakes, and lapses of others unfaithful to their call—drive nails into the body of Christ?

Kathryn and I agree that many Catholics in our country are not properly informed about the relevant issues facing the Church today. This is one of our biggest challenges, and it can be partially attributed to poor catechesis for a whole generation of Catholics. The Church is often scandalized and (as Kathryn describes) "awash with the muck of the darkness of our culture." She also thinks that often the case for the Church is not heard in the public square.

> We shy away from making the case, from offering to explain what exactly the Church proposes on the most neuralgic of issues. Very often we simply lack confidence. But the invitation to the sacraments is from God, and in his love we must be his messengers. Our time is short. What are we waiting for?

One of the obvious fruits of poor catechesis and not fully understanding our Catholic faith is the large numbers of Catholics who continue to vote for politicians who stand against several aspects of Church teaching. Kathryn says:

> All too often, we find ourselves happy to settle into ideological categories. Catholicism is not an ideology or party. Nor is it a nongovernmental organization, as Pope Francis has memorably said.
>
> It is a tremendous scandal that the Democratic party has become the reliable home of the abortion industry, given the number of Catholics who were leaders and members of

the party while this was happening. I'm currently reading Archbishop Gomez's recent book on immigration. In it, he makes the point that, while there isn't one Catholic solution to the political challenges we face on immigration, Catholics cannot afford to be indifferent on the issue. We cannot completely ignore the people who go to the 10:30 A.M. Spanish Mass. Parish communities that don't care for these "unfamiliar ones" aren't being Christian.

And the deepest wound on our national soul is abortion, legal for over forty years. What has each one of us done this week to make life seem a little more plausible to a desperate young single mother, to help support a couple who welcomed an unplanned child into the world? Do we support our neighbor's marriage as we work on ours? Is it any wonder we're a people who have no idea what marriage is anymore or what's different and wonderful about men and women, when even Catholics have lost the way in preaching and practice?

Perhaps part of the problem is where people choose to get their news and information. I asked Kathryn how to know what resources are appropriate for Catholics seeking accurate news related to the Church.

So much of the key to news consumption today has to do with the lens you choose. Does it clearly illuminate truth? Does the commentary educate and challenge? I am always trying to link to good lenses and clear my own! It's something we've tried to do on *NRO*, by having intelligent debates that people of good will are (and should be) having, and we all try to see more clearly and make constructive contributions. There's an urgency to this task, as everybody has finite time here on this earth, and we're going to have to answer for whether or not we were good stewards of the gifts we've been given.

Part of the "misinformation" about the Church comes from the way Pope Francis is being interpreted by the media. It is quite interesting to watch the media circus that often surrounds the Holy Father. Even Elton John chimed in with a comment for Italian *Vanity Fair* magazine, and he had admiring things to say about Pope Francis! Kathryn has firsthand insights into how Pope Francis is being covered by the media:

> Of course, so many praise Pope Francis with a focus on contrast. In *Lumen Fidei*, the letter to the Church and the entire world issued by Pope Francis and so clearly chiefly written by Pope Benedict, you see the continuity. The Church exists to bring people to Christ, to the reality of our call to live a Trinitarian reality, in union with God the Father, the Son, and the Holy Spirit. This call changes *everything*. It transforms us. That's what Pope Francis is about. I'm not sure that's entirely penetrated yet, even among those who attend Mass on Sundays. But he's sure drawing people in, and drawing them deeper. This is our moment in the Church to encounter Christ ourselves so that we might bring others to him through the way we live.
>
> *Lumen Fidei* is a snapshot of this papacy, reintroducing some basics and pleading that we believe—and know and love what we believe. Benedict was such a wonderful teacher,

but he knew we weren't fully hearing. He clearly prayed, and now Francis has the world's attention. *Lumen Fidei* amplifies the gifts of his predecessor, a master of catechesis. Will the world listen? We answer that by doing the spiritual equivalent of sitting up straighter: *pray.* How was your holy hour today? How was my Examen last night? During the papal visit to Washington, D.C., a few years ago, Metro ads taken out by the archdiocese quoted from *Spe Salvi:* "One who has hope lives differently" (2). Do we? What's keeping us from beginning now?

How does this busy woman with multiple roles fit prayer into her life? Kathryn says this is easy for her because she is tempted at times to become a hermit and only pray, but her schedule keeps that from happening. She is impressed and inspired by those who do whatever it takes to attend Mass each day despite their challenges at home and work. She says we all make time for a number of things, but the world needs us to pray more and make prayer a priority. Kathryn shared this final insight:

> I think if we *know* the secularization afoot, if we see the pain and suffering, if we see the practical atheism—especially in ourselves—we have a real responsibility to pray unceasingly, literally, giving every moment to the One who died for our eternal peace.

• THREE WAYS TO BE AN AUTHENTIC AND CANDID VOICE IN THE WORLD •

We are not all called to be writers or speakers like Kathryn Lopez, but we can learn valuable lessons from her on how to offer authentic and candid voices to support a new counterculture.

We must become the culture warriors. We have ample opportunity in our homes, schools, workplaces, bars, dorms, streets, and hospitals to care for those most in need, share the light of Christ with others, and offer an alternative way of life that is centered in Christ and not the secular world.

We must properly catechize ourselves. One of the key reasons Catholics support teachings counter to the Church and Christ's message in the Gospel is that they have not been well formed. We have an obligation to study our Catholic faith and know how to defend it with courage, conviction, and the living example of our own actions.

We must support and pray for our priests. Rather than criticize or be uncharitable toward our hardworking priests, we can instead pray for them. They have unbelievably difficult jobs and they deserve our help.

• QUESTIONS FOR REFLECTION •

1: Am I a culture warrior? How do I demonstrate through my words and actions that I stand for right and truth?

2: Who are the people I see in pain around me? What am I doing to show the love of Christ to them? For whom might I do something specific to lighten that person's burden?

3: How do I hear the call of the Holy Spirit in my life? Am I attentive in my prayers and discerning what I am being asked to do? What do I hear the Holy Spirit whispering to me?

4: How can I become more informed on topics relating to our Church? In what ways would this information affect my vote or support of public figures?

CHAPTER THIRTEEN

"Well Done, Good and Faithful Servant"
• THE LAITY ARE CALLED TO ACTION •

~~~

"By reason of their special vocation it belongs to the laity
to seek the kingdom of God by engaging in temporal affairs
and directing them according to God's will.... It pertains to
them in a special way so to illuminate and order all temporal
things with which they are closely associated that these may
always be effected and grow according to Christ and may be
to the glory of the Creator and Redeemer."

—*CCC* 898, quoting *Lumen Gentium*, 31

~~~

WHEN I ARRIVED AT THE CATHOLIC MARKETING NETWORK (CMN)
Conference in the summer of 2013, I was asked repeatedly if I
had met Alan Napleton. "Who is Alan Napleton?" I asked. He
was described to me as the guy in charge of CMN, one of the best
networked Catholics in the country, and one of the most faithful men
I would ever meet. Because of his hectic schedule and the demands of
the conference, we only had time for a brief handshake. But I stayed
in touch with this hardworking man and heard repeatedly from other
friends in the Catholic world what a tremendous asset he was to the
Church and what inspiration he provided to other laypeople to serve
God and make a positive difference in the world.

Alan Napleton grew up Catholic in a small blue-collar western Pennsylvania town, one of seven children. His parents were simple, hardworking people like their parents. They struggled a bit financially, always doing their best to provide for their children. The family had a strong work ethic, and from an early age Alan and his siblings held a variety of part-time jobs. Alan was determined to be the first in his family to graduate from college, and he achieved this through hard work, savings, and school loans.

After graduating with honors, he embarked on a business career that would take him to Amtrak, Ford Motor Company, and a large real estate development company. He did well in his career and realized the dreams of his parents and grandparents in terms of monetary achievement. However, all was not as it should have been at that time in his life.

> My spiritual life…was a different story; it was pretty much nonexistent. Although I had attended Catholic grammar school, I really did not know much about my faith. When I entered college and then the business world, I was much more interested in what the world had to offer, and I unfortunately began to live a sinful life—although at the time I didn't really have the spiritual maturity to even realize that what I was doing was sinful. Coming from a small town, now living in a large urban community with a great job, I wanted to "taste" what the world had to offer. Whatever faith I had at the time seemed to conflict with the materialistic lifestyle I was pursuing, and I stopped attending Mass.
>
> My career continued to thrive, and although my spiritual life was nonexistent, I thought I was doing pretty well. This all changed very dramatically in my late thirties, when

I had a profound religious experience brought about by Our Lady of Fatima. I had heard the story of Fatima from the good sisters when I was in the second or third grade, and it had made a big impact on me. I had pretty much forgotten the incident until, one day by chance, I came across a small pamphlet describing the occurrences at Fatima. Instantly the scales fell from my eyes, and I realized what I had been given the grace to realize as a young boy: that what had occurred at Fatima was true.

At the same time, I also realized that I was a child of God living in sin and that I was created for much more. Prior to picking up that pamphlet, I was focused like a laser on my career and climbing the corporate ladder. After reading it, I instantly lost all interest in both my career and all the false gods I had so ardently pursued.

Although friends and family understandably questioned my decision, I managed to muster the faith and courage to walk away from that career and begin a life's work that hopefully will lead me home to my heavenly Father. I know without a shadow of doubt that the direction I was going prior to that dramatic awakening would have led to eternal disaster. For the blessing and gift of that awakening, I thank the Lord and his Blessed Mother every day.

Life Turned Upside Down

Alan's changed perspective on life had a significant effect on him and all who knew him. Alan was almost forty at the time and still single, although he was living with a girl he had known for several years. Alan carefully explained to her what had occurred in his life, and although religion and faith hadn't been something they had discussed, she seemed supportive, to Alan's great surprise. After executing a difficult exit from the corporate world, he asked his girlfriend to marry him, bought a house, and began a journey with a very unclear destination.

Relying on his savings, Alan did volunteer work for two years with local Catholic charities and pro-life organizations. He and his wife wanted to start a family. When they discovered that they were unable to have children of their own, they began the process to adopt a child.

Our Lady of Fatima had been the catalyst for Alan's spiritual awakening, and now Our Lady of Guadalupe began to play a significant role in his spiritual life. The path to a new career became clearer. Alan explains:

> I've gone to the Our Lady of Guadalupe Shrine in Mexico City probably fifty times in the last two decades and have received many blessings through this devotion. Some twenty-two years ago, I met a group of Mexican businessmen at the shrine who were producing high-quality children's videos on the lives of the saints. It was a wonderful ministry/business, and they were looking for someone to run their operation in the United States. My savings were beginning to run out, so I accepted their offer and thus began my work with Catholic distribution and the Catholic Marketing Network.

But just as his future career was launched and life at home seemed ideal, Alan received the biggest shock of his life.

> After five years of marriage and prayer to Our Lady of Guadalupe, we adopted a beautiful baby boy from Mexico City. I was never happier. I was in love with my wife and my new son. Although my job didn't pay much, I loved what I was doing. That all came to an abrupt end one day, when I

came home from work to a note from my wife telling me that she had left me, taking my son with her. I thought we were happily married, but she believed I had become a religious fanatic. I soon found out that there was another man involved, and I was introduced to the reality of no-fault divorce. Within five months we were divorced, and my now ex-wife quickly remarried and moved several hundred miles away. Fortunately I obtained joint custody of my son, and although it was a challenge with the distance, we have remained close. He has been a source of great joy in my life.

I was very traumatized by this turn of events. At the time I was very hurt (in fact, I was not sure I was going to survive) and confused, but I never felt abandoned by God. In fact, my faith provided me with the comfort I so desperately needed as I slowly began a healing process that continues to this day.

It is often in the midst of great tragedy and suffering that God provides peace and the courage to serve him in ways that bring blessings for ourselves and others. It was during this low point that the Lord began opening several doors for Alan, and he found himself involved in a number of Catholic projects. He also encountered some very holy people who helped him realize and appreciate the fact that he had been given the privilege of working in God's vineyard in a special way.

I continue to thank the Lord for this privilege, and it would be difficult for me to explain how many wonderful spiritual blessings I have witnessed and experienced in my own life and the lives of others over the past two decades. I have come to realize how much each of us depends on God and how much he loves us and is always there for us, especially in times of trial. I am grateful that he has allowed me to work with many wonderful people of faith on many different Church-related projects. My deepening faith is a source of great joy for me, and although it's certainly not easy at times, I have tried to turn my life completely over to God as he leads me on my journey through life.

Alan's story is compelling on many levels, not the least of which are his complete trust in God to see him through a torturous time in his personal life and his dedication to God and the Church. I asked Alan to reflect on his work and share what are the unmet needs of the Church that he tries to address.

This is a very exciting time to be a lay Catholic. The Church is calling on the laity to play an important role in the life of the Church and the New Evangelization; we've heard Popes Francis, Benedict, and John Paul II repeatedly sound this call to action. The laity is being challenged, young and old, to bring a new zeal and vigor to the work of spreading Christ's Gospel, and in some small way I have tried my best to respond to this clarion call.

As I look back over the past two decades, I can honestly say that I have not had much of a plan or tried to address any particular need, but rather I have simply walked through the doors Christ has opened. In doing so I have stayed very busy, working on a number of wonderful Church-related projects. I have also been given the additional blessing of meeting and working with a number of exemplary fellow Christians who have edified and strengthened me through the example of their Christ-centered lives.

I am now in my mid-sixties, and like each of us, I do not know whether Christ will give me another twenty minutes or twenty years of life. I have been blessed with good health, and Lord willing, I will use the health and energy I continue to have to work on whatever projects God puts in front of me. I also realize that activity alone, no matter how good the cause, does not necessarily bring one closer to God, and people can fall into the trap of staying so busy that they neglect their prayer lives and other important obligations and relationships. Going forward, I want to strive for a better balance of activity that also serves to deepen my personal spiritual life. There will also be plenty of unmet needs to work on, but I think the one the Lord calls me and all of us to is the need to become saints. It's rather easy to stay very busy with worthwhile projects—it's much more difficult to make meaningful progress toward our sanctity.

Alan Napleton's days are consumed with leading a number of organizations and projects. In light of his hectic pace, I appreciate his understanding that activity alone will not bring one closer to God. How does he stay grounded in his Catholic faith? What habits has he developed over the years to help in this effort?

Cultivating patience is one key thing; I have learned to wait on the Lord in all things while trying to keep my eyes and mind focused on Christ in every moment and in every situation. Also, learning to trust in God's providence has a natural outcome of worrying less. I have come to a better understanding of the value of prayer and spending more time in "conversation" with God, attending and participating in

Holy Mass, and especially taking advantage of the great gift of Eucharistic Adoration.

Like Alan, many of us endure painful personal challenges and obstacles in our lives that may negatively affect our faith. Alan is an inspiration to us all for the way he turned the darkest time in his life into a blessing. I asked Alan if it is possible that God called him to all the good work he is doing in the Catholic world as a way to ease his personal pain.

> Certainly God can bring good out of any bad, and my divorce is no exception. We know that God hates divorce, and having experienced this tragedy firsthand, I sometimes find it difficult to see how any good could come from such an evil.

> But as time has passed and the pain has eased, I have seen that perhaps good may have come from what occurred—that the Lord has used my failed marriage in some mysterious way to accomplish his will. I didn't want the divorce, but I couldn't stop it. Although it was a heart-wrenching, terrible experience, perhaps it has allowed me to continue working for the Church. That work has brought me a great deal of joy and comfort, and I can't imagine doing anything else. This benefit has also played out in the life of my nineteen-year-old son. Because of my work, he has been exposed to many aspects, individuals, and leaders of the Church, and I believe those experiences have had a very positive influence on his life and spiritual development, and that has been a wonderful blessing for both of us.

For Alan Napleton, the last two decades have produced an impressive body of work in the service of Christ and the Church. I asked this humble man if he ever reflected on his legacy.

> It's an interesting question, but upon reflection I can honestly say that I have never thought of my legacy. My great desire and hope is that when I am standing in front of the Lord, I might hear him say, "Well done, good and faithful servant." My heart leaps at just the thought that might occur!
>
> But all of us will be remembered, and I would hope that loved ones, friends, and associates will remember me as a simple man who loved his Catholic faith, tried to respond to God's call to serve him, and was a man of prayer. I ask God every day to make me such a man, and although I am certainly not there yet, it is something that I strive for. As I take small steps in deepening my prayer life, I am beginning to realize its power. Prayer has brought me closer to God and made me more at peace.

• FOUR WAYS THE LAITY CAN ANSWER GOD'S CALL TO ACTION •
Alan's story contains great lessons about overcoming the materialism of the secular world, awakening spiritually, dealing with adversity, being open to God's will in our lives, and staying focused on our Catholic faith. Here are four critical teachings we can make use of in our own lives.

God can turn any adversity into something good if we trust him. All of us have likely encountered some kind of serious adversity. We can turn to God in these difficult times and ask for help instead of relying on our own strength. We can exercise complete faith in his divine providence, knowing that everything will work out. When faced with obstacles, we should turn to him in prayer and ask for strength, courage, and peace, always remembering that we are blessed with a heavenly Father who loves us.

Ask the Blessed Mother to help us. Alan's spiritual awakening through prayers to Our Lady of Fatima and Our Lady of Guadalupe demonstrate the power of the Blessed Mother's intercession. We too can reflect on the miracles and messages of Our Lady at Fatima and Guadalupe and pray to the Blessed Mother for help and comfort. She will always hear us and provide the assistance we need.

Remember that activity alone does not bring one closer to God. It is easy to think that our nonprofit work, contributions to the parish community, and other Church-related efforts are enough. We must be careful to not confuse our well-intended "busyness" with growing closer in our relationship with God. Daily prayer, daily Mass, and time in Eucharistic Adoration should also be part of our efforts, with the goal of growing in sanctity outweighing the works of our hands.

Think of your legacy as the Lord's saying, "Well done, good and faithful servant." The choices we make now will determine whether we lead the kind of life that will merit these words someday. It's never too late to begin, and our passion for God can grow stronger with each passing year.

• QUESTIONS FOR REFLECTION •

1: How have I dealt with adversity in my life? Did I trust in God? How did God transform my challenges into blessings?

2: Alan shared that he was simply open to what God had in store for him. In my life, am I truly open to God's will and plan? What am I discerning these days about how I can best serve God and others?

3: Do I see serving others as a privilege or a burden? Do I grudgingly give my time and energy to good causes, or do I participate out of guilt or peer pressure? What steps can I take to develop more of a servant's heart?

4: In my desire to serve and give back, am I neglecting my spiritual life? Where do I see the need for more balance between being active in Church projects and spending time in prayer, alone with God? Is becoming a saint truly my goal, or am I focused on less important things? What do I need to let go of? What stands in the way of my spiritual growth?

Regular Catholic Heroes
• CAN WE DO SOMETHING EXTRAORDINARY FOR GOD? •

DO WE FEEL LET DOWN BY POLITICIANS AND PUBLIC FIGURES WHO SAY they are Catholic but whose words and actions are often contrary to the teachings of the Church? Do we seek good examples for ourselves, our children, and our grandchildren to emulate, because we hope such examples will demonstrate in word and deed what it means to be authentically Catholic? Perhaps we are looking in the wrong places. Maybe for too long we have placed the wrong people on pedestals. It is entirely possible that we need look no further than our own parishes, workplaces, and communities for what I like to call "regular Catholic heroes."

As you have learned through the many examples in this book, regular Catholic heroes abound, but we may fail to notice them. It is easy to overlook the faithful, virtuous, humble, and selfless among us. Perhaps we are not aware of them because they go about serving Christ and his Church in quiet ways, avoiding the spotlight as much as possible. They care more about serving others than about getting credit for their efforts. When they are not working, they are likely to be spending quality time with their families, serving others in the community, or on their knees in prayer. They provide powerful and joyful witness in the simplest of actions—and that makes them extraordinary.

Over the past several years, I have been blessed to encounter several people who I think fit the definition of Catholic heroes. In addition to the extraordinary Catholics you have encountered in *Joyful Witness*, three people in particular are continually good role models for me and others. *Tom*, a senior sales leader committed to the Church and his family, selflessly gives his time to a local homeless shelter and organizes our parish community to support it. He is a prayer warrior who loves the rosary and can always be counted on when you need help. *Paige*, a senior executive with an Atlanta-based company, is a devoted Catholic wife and mother who finds time to carry out her business duties, run a jobs ministry at her parish, teach parish religion classes, and selflessly help anyone she meets to find everything from stronger faith to a new job. Finally there is *Brian*, a model husband and father of four children who is one of the most faithful Catholics I have ever met. He is the behind-the-scenes organizer who makes sure things get done in his parish, and he shuns the limelight. All three of these people inspire me in numerous ways to be a better Catholic. Ironically, they would be very uncomfortable being described as inspirational heroes, and they see nothing extraordinary in the ways they live and serve.

• RECOGNIZING REGULAR CATHOLIC HEROES •

• They clearly show the light of Christ to those around them.
• They are joyful and make being Catholic look inviting and attractive.
• They follow the Magisterium and are devoted to the sacraments.
• They have vibrant prayer lives.
• They live authentic Catholic lives that don't change to suit their companions or to avoid challenges.
• When dealing with others, they are always about the other and not about themselves.
• It is their privilege to do any task necessary to help a ministry or to serve another person.

• They possess a quiet and powerful form of courage in the face of adversity, which emanates from their complete trust in Jesus Christ.

These humble and selfless Catholic heroes all around us may be the saints of tomorrow. We should seek them out, share our sincere gratitude, and pray that we will be able to follow their great example.

Are we ready to do whatever it takes to share our own joyful witness and become Catholic heroes to the people we encounter each day?

I hope this book has encouraged you to desire more than an ordinary Catholic life—just going through the motions instead of truly living your faith. My hope is that you have found inspiration, hope, and practical ideas from the men and women featured in this book and that you will find your own ways to live an extraordinary Catholic life. We are called to be holy, and we are made for heaven. Nothing less than an extraordinary Catholic life will suffice!

Pope Francis on Following Christ, Experiencing the Joy of the Gospel, and Living the Catholic Faith

"We must not be afraid of being Christian and living as Christians! We must have this courage to go and proclaim the Risen Christ, for he is our peace. He made peace with his love, with his forgiveness, with his blood, and with his mercy." (*Regina Coeli*, April 7, 2013)

"The joy of the gospel fills the hearts and lives of all who encounter Jesus. Those who accept his offer of salvation are set free from sin, sorrow, inner emptiness, and loneliness. With Christ joy is constantly born anew." (*Evangelii Gaudium*, 1)

"I invite all Christians, everywhere, at this very moment, to a renewed personal encounter with Jesus Christ, or at least an openness to letting him encounter them; I ask all of you to do this unfailingly each day. No one should think that this invitation is not meant for him or her, since 'no one is excluded from the joy brought by the Lord.'" (*Evangelii Gaudium*, 3, quoting *Gaudete in Domino*, 297)

"Ours is not a joy born of having many possessions, but from having encountered a Person: Jesus, in our midst; it is born from knowing that with him we are never alone, even at difficult moments, even when our life's journey comes up against problems and obstacles that seem insurmountable, and there are so many of them! And in this moment the enemy, the devil, comes, often disguised as an angel, and slyly speaks his word to us. Do not listen to him! Let us follow Jesus!" (Homily, World Youth Day, March 24, 2013)

"Following and accompanying Christ, staying with him, demands 'coming out of ourselves'…out of a dreary way of living faith that has become a habit, out of the temptation to withdraw into our own plans, which end by shutting out God's creative action." (General Audience, March 27, 2013)

"Christ opened the path to us. He is like a roped guide climbing a mountain, who on reaching the summit, pulls us up to him and leads us to God. If we entrust our life to him, if we let ourselves be guided by him, we are certain to be in safe hands, in the hands of our Saviour, of our Advocate." (General Audience, April 17, 2013)

"To be sure, the testimony of faith comes in very many forms, just as in a great fresco there is a variety of colours and shades yet they are all important, even those which do not stand out. In God's great plan, every detail is important, even yours, even my humble little witness, even the hidden witness of those who live their faith with simplicity in everyday family relationships, work relationships, friendships.... Let us all remember this: one cannot proclaim the Gospel of Jesus without the tangible witness of one's life. Those who listen to us and observe us must be able to see in our actions what they hear from our lips, and so give glory to God!" (Homily, April 14, 2013)

"May you also be true evangelizers! May your initiatives be 'bridges,' means of bringing others to Christ, so as to journey together with him. And in this spirit may you always be attentive to charity. Each individual Christian and every community is missionary to the extent that they bring to others and live the Gospel, and testify to God's love for all, especially those experiencing difficulties." (Homily, May 5, 2013)

"We too should be clear in our Christian life that entering the glory of God demands daily fidelity to his will, even when it demands sacrifice and sometimes requires us to change our plans." (General Audience, April 17, 2013)

Sharing the Joy of Our Faith with Everyone,
Even the Angry and Upset

As joyful witnesses, we are called to share the joy of our faith with *everyone*, and sometimes that includes Catholics who have fallen away from their faith. It might mean talking about our faith with Catholics who are angry and bitter toward the Church. Their reasons may vary, but how we engage with them may mean the difference between their possible return to the Church and losing them forever.

I encountered one such person not long ago.

As a favor to a client, I met for lunch with a visiting business executive who wanted to relocate to Atlanta from another area of the country and needed help with her job search. When our food and coffee arrived, I invited her to join me in a blessing of the meal, and I made the Sign of the Cross. I noticed that she gave me a funny look when I finished, but I ignored it and moved into the discussion. As I advised her on various ways she could connect with other leaders and job opportunities in our area, I mentioned how "faith-friendly" the Southeast is, and I told her that discussing faith, family, and anything else she wanted when building new relationships was likely easier than it was where she was currently living. I received my second funny look and had to respond.

"I noticed you seemed a little unsettled when I said the blessing and mentioned how easy it is to discuss faith and personal things in our area. I was trying to prepare and encourage you regarding building your network—I did not intend to make you uncomfortable."

Her response was very measured, with a tinge of anger. "I am also Catholic, although I haven't been active in quite a few years. I have too many issues with the Church and all of its problems, and I just can't overlook them."

To be honest, I was a little nervous when I asked, "Would you like to discuss what the issues are?"

Reluctantly, she said, "I don't like some of the decisions the Church has made on marriage, contraception, and other social issues. I still can't get over the sex-abuse scandals. I know there are a lot of people who agree with me."

Here was the moment of truth. Do I defend the Church? Change the subject?

Saying a quick prayer to the Blessed Mother, I opted to engage with her. I summarize my comments; in essence I said, "I am really grateful that you shared this with me. I realize you are going through a difficult time with these faith issues, finding a new job, and moving to a new city. This is a lot to handle! You might find it interesting that, before I converted to the Catholic Church, I spent over two decades in the spiritual wilderness, with no faith at all, dating from when I left the Baptist church as a teenager. One of the many things that drew me to the Church's teaching was that I knew in my heart that what I was learning was *true*. I was blown away as I learned more and more about the Church Christ founded.

"When I began to see St. Peter as the first pope, it dawned on me that he was a sinful man who denied Christ three times, and yet he still was chosen to lead the Church. He was forgiven. I felt there was surely hope for me and everyone else! Reading the lives of the saints and the writings of St. John Paul II were also transformative for me. I remember someone sharing a quote from Dr. Peter Kreeft that connects back to what you have said: 'The Church is a hospital for sinners, not a museum for saints.'

"I know you are angry and frustrated. I promise you I really do understand. But there is so much good in the Church, and there are many holy men and women in it who work and pray every day for our salvation. There are also sinful people who have done horrible things. We are still called to love and forgive them, as difficult as it may be.

"With regard to your disagreement with Catholic teaching on marriage and contraception, don't you find it somewhat comforting that the Church has *not* changed its teaching to suit the modern world? While other religious denominations cave in to cultural pressures, the Catholic Church remains strong and consistent in defending the truth, despite the abhorrent behavior of a tiny percentage of its priests. I would encourage you to focus on Christ and the lessons he teaches us through the Gospels. Read about the lives of the saints. Seek the intercession of the Blessed Mother to help you forgive. Pray to Christ for help and strength as well as understanding and the capacity for forgiveness. You and I are flawed sinners. What if nobody ever forgave us for the mistakes we have committed (and will commit in the future)?"

She was silent for a few minutes before saying something that surprised me: "I respect what you have said and appreciate your not avoiding the topic. I'm not sure I feel better, but I will think and pray about this and see what happens. I certainly didn't expect this conversation during our lunch!"

Nothing radical occurred. I said nothing earth-shattering, and she wasn't suddenly ready to rush back into the arms of the Church. What *did* happen is that we had a discussion about something painful for her. She vented, I listened, and I offered her my own very positive witness and experience with the Catholic Church in response. One of the wonderful things about this conversation was her willingness to listen and not get angry and leave. She agreed to pray and think about what I shared with her. I think the anger and frustration may have come down a notch, and with prayers (hers, mine, and yours), she may just return to the Church. I followed up with an e-mail offering to discuss this subject anytime and letting her know that I would pray for her.

When we encounter someone who is angry with the Church, it's not our place to preach or judge. Instead, patiently listen. We can offer them a positive alternative to their anger through our own joyful experiences with Christ and his Church. Pray for them in earnest, and let the Holy Spirit go to work on bringing them back into the fold. This conversation made me reflect, as perhaps we all should, on the many people all around us with similar issues whom we never identify or engage in a loving dialogue. Food for thought.

> What man of you, having a hundred sheep, if he has lost one of them, does not leave the ninety-nine in the wilderness, and go after the one which is lost, until he finds it? And when he has found it, he lays it on his shoulders rejoicing. And when he comes home, he calls together his friends and his neighbors, saying to them, "Rejoice with me, for I have found my sheep which was lost." Just so, I tell you, there will be more joy in heaven over one sinner who repents than over ninety-nine righteous persons who have no need of repentance. (Luke 15:4–7)

Four Simple Steps to Joy

The early Christians had the good fortune to be the first to share the Good News. Imagine the joy they felt in sharing Christ's message of love with everyone! They stood out as happy in a suffering world, just as Christians have the opportunity to do today. Jesus promised the apostles (and us) this joy at the Last Supper: "So you have sorrow now, but I will see you again, and your hearts will rejoice, and no one will take your joy from you" (John 16:22).

Do we show our joy at home, at work, with friends? We have so much to be truly thankful for in our relationship with Christ and the truth and beauty of our Catholic faith. Being truly joyful should lead to sharing that joy and expressing the truths of our faith to others in a way that shows the depth of our belief and love.

St. Paul reinforces the call to be joyful in 1 Thessalonians 5:16–18: "Rejoice always, pray constantly, give thanks in all circumstances; for this is the will of God in Christ Jesus for you." Paul makes it sound simple, so why do we struggle to do something that appears to be so easy? We all deal with various forms of adversity. Some of us are unemployed, some are dealing with illness, and others are struggling with relationship or financial problems. The encroachments on our religious freedom and unwarranted attacks on the Church have made many Catholics gloomy and frightened. These are real obstacles to joy, and they must be acknowledged. But as Romans 12:12 says: "Rejoice in your hope, be patient in tribulation."

As tough as things may be, Catholics have work to do for Christ. Like the early Christians, we too are called to share the Good News. Do you recall that during St. Paul's life, he was shipwrecked, imprisoned, beaten, starved, and stoned (see 2 Corinthians 11:23–27)? He showed incredible courage and fortitude in sharing his joy and the message of Christ with the Gentiles despite his suffering. We are called to follow his example today.

For Catholics, joy in the midst of extreme adversity is our obligation and our duty. Remember that we are not alone. Our faith in Christ and our devotion to the sacraments that bind us to him will see us through the tough times and help us share a joy that will not evaporate in the face of tough challenges. Be encouraged by our Lord's words in John 16:33: "I have said this to you, that in me you may have peace. In the world you have tribulation; but be of good cheer, I have overcome the world."

It is easy to get lost in our problems and forget to be joyful—it happens to me and just about everyone else I know. But remember that we are surrounded by people who are watching us. They may be seeking him and looking for someone, anyone, to show them the way to Christ. They could learn from our good example, be inspired by our joy, and be encouraged by our faith journey, if we will only remember that we are called to share the Good News. If we are gloomy, frustrated, inward-focused, and critical of the Church, we will never be able to help anyone, and we may even put our own salvation at risk.

Let me leave you with four simple actions I try to do in my desire to be joyful. This is by no means a definitive list, and I would love to learn what others are doing. But here is what often works for me:

I surrender to Christ every day. I recommit to putting him first in all areas of my life.

I release my burdens to Jesus in daily prayer. I can't do it alone, and I need his help!

I am thankful for my blessings. Rather than dwell on my problems, I focus on all of the incredible blessings in my life and express my gratitude in prayer.

I start with the end in mind. Will Jesus be able to say to me one day, "Well done, good and faithful servant"? Are my actions each day serving him?

Do you find it difficult or easy to share your joy? I think Cardinal Timothy Dolan of New York sums it up well: "Being Catholic is not a heavy burden, snuffing the joy out of life; rather our faith in Jesus and His Church gives meaning, purpose and joy to life."[3]

---

3. Archbishop Timothy Dolan, "It's a blessing to be here: Why I'm proud to lead the wonderful Archdiocese of New York," *Daily News,* April 15, 2009, www.nydailynews.com.